OPENING THE SPACE FRONTIER

SPACE EXPLORATION

OPENING THE
SPACE FRONTIER

Ray Spangenburg
and
Diane Moser

Facts On File

New York • Oxford

Opening the Space Frontier

Facts On File, Inc.   Facts On FIle Limited
460 Park Avenue South or   Collins Street
New York NY 10016   Oxford ox4 1xJ
USA   United Kingdom

Library of Congress Cataloging-in-Publication Data

Spangenburg, Ray, 1939-
    Opening the space frontier/by Ray Spangenburg and Diane Moser.
       p. cm. — (Space exploration; 1)
    Bibliography: p.
    Includes index.
    ISBN 0-8160-1848-0 (alk. paper). $22.95
    1. Outer Space—Exploration—History. 2. Rocketry—History.
I. Moser, Diane, 1988- . II. Title. III. Series.
TL788.5.S65 1989
639.45'009—dc19

British CIP data available on request from Facts On File.

Facts On File books are available at special discounts when purchased
in bulk quantities for businesses, associations, institutions, or sales
promotion. Please contact the Special Sales Department of our New
York office at 212/683-2244 (dial 800/322-8755 except in NY, AK or HI).

Text and Jacket design by Ron Monteleone
Composition by Facts On File, Inc.
Manufactured by Maple-Vail Book Manufacturing Group
Printed in the United States of America

Front jacket illustration: Gemini 7 as seen from Gemini 6 (NASA)
Back jacket illustration: Astronaut Ed White's spacewalk during Gemini 4
mission (Nasa)
10 9 8 7 6 5 4 3 2 1

This book is printed on acid-free paper.

CONTENTS

Preface   vii

Acknowledgments   viii

Introduction   ix

PART ONE: THE EARLY YEARS   1

Chapter 1:   Visions of Space Travel: The Long-standing Dream   3
Chapter 2:   Blasting Off: The Early Development of Rocketry   6
     BOX: What is a Rocket?   9
Chapter 3:   Weaponry or Wizardry? The German V-2 Rocket   13
     BOX: German Rocketry to 1945   17
Chapter 4:   Advancing on Space: Rocket Development 1945-1957   20
     BOX: U.S. Rocketry to 1957   25
     BOX: Soviet Rocketry to 1957   26
Chapter 5:   Sputnik and Explorer 1 Begin the Space Age: 1957-1960   29
     BOX: Milestones in Space: The Sputnik Era, 1957-1960   32

PART TWO: SENDING HUMANS INTO SPACE   35

Chapter 6:   Wings Toward Space: The Story of the X-15   37
     BOX: Mach 1 and the "Sonic Barrier"   38
Chapter 7:   The First Humans in Space: Vostok and Mercury   42
     BOX: Milestones in Space: Vostok and Mercury, 1961-1963   49
     BOX: The Vostok Spacecraft   49
     BOX: The Mercury Spacecraft   50
Chapter 8:   More, Farther, Longer: Voskhod and Gemini   52
     BOX: The Voskhod Spacecraft   53
     BOX: The Gemini Spacecraft   56
     BOX: The Agena Target Vehicle   60
     BOX: Milestones in Space: The Gemini and Voskhod Years, 1964-1966   63
Chapter 9:   1967: A Bad Year for Space   65
     BOX: Profiles in Courage   67
Chapter 10:   Shooting for the Moon: The Early Apollo Years, 1968-1969   69
     BOX: The Saturn V Rocket   69
     BOX: The Apollo Spacecraft   73
     BOX: Milestones in Space: The Apollo Years, 1967-1972   77

Chapter 11: Soyuz: Long-term Passport to Space   79
BOX: The Soyuz Spacecraft   80
BOX: Milestones in Space: Soyuz Missions, 1967-1971   83

PART THREE: TAKING THE GIANT STEP TO THE MOON   85

Chapter 12: "The Eagle Has Landed": Apollo 11   87
BOX: The Lunar Module   89
Chapter 13: Exploring the Moon: Apollo 12-17   94

Appendix: Pioneers in Space   101

Glossary   102

Suggestions For Further   105
Reading

Index   107

PREFACE

The vast expanse of space has long beckoned, but only during the last half of the 20th century have we developed the ability to venture there ourselves, sent probes far into the solar system and beyond, and set new technologies toward the vastness of our universe to explore the stars in new and revealing ways. Space has been called the final frontier—and in a sense it is the last and ultimate destination of explorers. It is a region that tests our ingenuity and courage, our spirit of survival, and our wisdom and understanding.

SPACE EXPLORATION is a series of four books that follows humankind's adventures in space. *Opening the Space Frontier* tells the story of the first space scientists to dare to believe we could reach space from Earth; the engineers who experimented and built rockets that could soar beyond the atmosphere; the test pilots who flew experimental planes traveling faster than sound and zooming 50 miles high and more; and those first humans who bravely traveled in the great vacuum beyond our atmosphere. It relates both the exciting early Soviet and American triumphs and the losses in manned space exploration.

Other books in the series continue the saga with the still-unfolding story of space exploration and commercialization today (*Living and Working in Space*); a close look at the mysteries of the Solar System uncovered by planetary probes like the Voyager, VEGA, and Viking missions (*Exploring the Reaches of the Solar System*); and close-ups of the lives of space pioneers from the beginning to the present (*Space People from A-Z*).

Together, these volumes tell an exciting tale of human endeavor at its best—dreaming dreams, solving problems and achieving results. Civilization today owes much to the pioneers and those who continue to venture—both personally, in manned programs, and intellectually, through their contributions to technology—into space.

ACKNOWLEDGMENTS

This book could never have happened without the help of countless individuals in both industry and government throughout the world. While we won't try to name them all, we appreciate the time so many took to provide photographs, drawings and information. A few stand out as extraordinary, and to them a special "thank you": to Terry White, formerly of NASA's Johnson Space Center, for his memory of more than 25 years of American manned space exploration; to Mike Gentry at JSC for his knack for locating photos; and to Nick Johnson at Teledyne Brown Engineering for his generous contribution of drawings and information on the Soviet program. Also to four magazine editors whose curious minds have kept us covering a steady stream of fascinating assignments on space over the years: Tony Reichhardt of *Final Frontier*, John Rhea, formerly of *Space World*, and Kate McMains and Leonard David of *Ad Astra*. And for their supportive enthusiasm, to our agent, Linda Allen; and to James Warren and Deirdre Mullane, our editors at Facts On File. Without you all this book would not be.

INTRODUCTION

Throughout time, we humans have sought far beyond the horizons's limits for the next frontier, and the next, and the next. Always questing with curious minds, we send our thoughts, like space ships, probing the vast unknown, searching constantly to know and understand. Turning inward, we seek to understand ourselves, turning outward, to understand the world around us.

As we go about our daily lives, our immediate world seems enormous and complex—complicated enough to occupy all our thoughts, filled with enough problems and puzzles to last many lifetimes. But standing alone at night, backing away from the hustle and bustle, like generations before us, we look to the skies. In those moments we know that the world is more than our experience of it, that the world is and always has been everything the human mind can dream, and more. The human imagination stretches from Earth to the farthest, most distant stars.

The story of humankind's quest beyond Earth's cocoon into space begins far back with those first lone individuals who looked up into the night, wondering. It gained momentum with Galileo Galilei's construction and use of a telescope to view the planets in 1609, and surged into the 20th century on those twin bridges of human genius—ambitious vision and pragmatic engineering. These pages recount the exciting story of those beginnings: the development of rockets and the triumphs that followed from the first human-made satellite to the first human step on the Moon.

*To the first pioneers who ventured into
space, all those who helped them get there,
and all those who dreamed it possible . . . .*

*To the men and women at NASA,
dreamers and doers all . . . .*

And, as forever, to P.J.

PART 1

THE EARLY YEARS

1

VISIONS
OF SPACE TRAVEL:
THE LONG-STANDING DREAM

The Far Horizon and Beyond

We'll never know what the first humans thought when they looked up to the night skies or what they imagined the stars to be. Perhaps, huddled in their caves, seeking shelter against the fall of night and its shadowy terrors, those early minds, preoccupied with survival, remained always more intent on the snapping of a twig, the breathing in the bushes, the cry in the darkness. Later would come the wondering, the mythologies, the gods. How hard it must have been in that early darkness merely to wait for the dawn.

Inevitably, though, the dawn did come. With it each day the human mind reached a little farther and stretched to understand just a little bit more. Over the long years, decades, centuries, humanity slowly found room to puzzle over new mysteries. We developed solutions to those mysteries in the form of wondrous tales, handed down orally from generation to generation—tales of heroes and gods, the world and nature. And inevitably, too, tales of the Sun, Moon and the stars that seemed to play such an important role in the cycles of human existence.

As human consciousness expanded to encompass more and more of nature and history by way of myth and legends, it also reached out toward more scientific explanations of the world's mysteries. By 3000 B.C. the Babylonians had begun making careful observations of the heavens. Soon the Egyptians had developed a calendar and the first catalog of the stars. In a rapid historical kaleidoscope of activity that began around the early sixth century B.C., the Greeks developed ideas, charts, tables and philosophical explanations for the motions of the Sun, Moon and stars and they brought the heavens into everyday consciousness.

Imaginary Voyages

As the heavens became more familiar, they began to be seen as a *place* that one might even visit. Of course, getting there took some imagination.

Projectile aiming for the Moon from Jules Verne's *From the Earth to the Moon* (1847 edition)

It was by storytellers and writers that people were first taken to the far-flung stars and planets. One of the earliest writers to talk about space travel was the Greek philosopher Lucian of Somosata. Writing in the first century A.D., Lucian was more interested in the moral of his stories than their realism. Getting from the Earth to the Moon was managed with the help of a powerful whirlwind in one tale and by having his heroes strap on wings and jump upward from a mountaintop in another.

Early writers like Lucian and others who followed in the centuries to come were, after all, writing tales of the imagination, not textbooks on physics. Sixteenth-century Italian writer Lodovico Ariosto included a journey to the Moon in a story he wrote, and so did 17th-century German astronomer Johannes Kepler. Both devised highly imaginative means for getting to the Moon—a horse-drawn chariot for Ariosto and demons for Kepler. When Savinien de Cyrano de Bergerac (French adventurer, poet, writer and swordsman) wrote a story called *Voyage to the Moon* in 1649, he wove a rollicking tale about an extraordi-

nary attempt to reach the Moon by tying bottles of dew to his body. When the sun came out, he reasoned, the dew would rise and so would he.

In the 18th century, several French satirists described fictional people on other planets as a way, by use of comparison and contrast, to criticize their own culture's customs and mores. However, as the 18th century drew to a close, a growing body of scientific knowledge began to make readers more skeptical of such farfetched schemes as trips to the Moon and planets using a horse-drawn chariot or evaporating dew. Still, since no one had yet imagined any realistic way of getting human beings off the ground and into space, the imaginative speculation continued.

The Birth of Science Fiction

The earliest science-fiction stories—fiction that centers around the futuristic, imaginative possibilities of science and technology—probably dates

Space travelers returning to Earth after a fantastic balloon ride through space (from Jules Verne's *Hector Servadac or Off on a Comet*, 1877 edition)

4

back to an 18th-century tale about a visitor from the planet Mercury who arrives on Earth by way of an electric flying machine. The use of a *technological* device (though still not a very plausible one) for space travel was significant.

Others followed in the early 19th century, but it was French writer Jules Verne who really put the *science* in science fiction when he wrote *From the Earth to the Moon*, published in 1865, followed by *Around the Moon* in 1870.

With a vivid and lively imagination and a fine storytelling talent, Jules Verne had a gift for sketching tales of science and technology that were often quite accurate—or, failing that, at least sounded accurate. Strongly plotted and concerned as much with story and colorful characterization as with scientific der-ring-do, his work was a great popular success and more importantly it had an enormous influence on early space and rocketry pioneers worldwide. Most of the great rocket pioneers would later read Verne and more than one would credit the prolific French writer's works for inspiration.

If Jules Verne, still read and enjoyed today, was the grandfather of science fiction, then its father is certainly H. G. Wells. Born in England in 1866, Wells was a child of the Industrial Revolution, a time when the replacement of hand tools by power tools and mechanized production brought about massive social and economic changes. He was a strong supporter, and occasionally a cautionary critic, of the march of science and technology. His relentlessly curious, probing and intelligent mind produced a body of work that entertained and informed many thousands of readers in his own time and ours.

War of the Worlds, serialized in magazines in 1897, *The First Men in the Moon*, published in 1901, and many other works of science and science speculation, including *The Invisible Man* (1897) and *The Time Machine* (1895), showed the wonders, excitement and dangers of science and technology to the average reader as never before.

Always attuned to the latest developments of scientific and philosophic thought, by the time of his death in 1946 at the age of 79, Wells had witnessed not only the advent of a new age of science and technology but the horror of two world wars. The second of those wars saw the streets of London exploding daily under the assaults of devastating and deadly rockets.

Ironically, it was the power of those same rockets that would change the world forever, directing its vision outward toward the age of space, the Moon, planets and the stars.

2

BLASTING OFF: THE EARLY DEVELOPMENT OF ROCKETRY

Aiming at the stars, both literally and figuratively, is a problem to occupy generations, so that no matter how much progress one makes, there is always the thrill of just beginning.
—Robert Goddard
American rocket pioneer

China and the Beginnings of Rocketry

Sometime more than 800 years or so ago, someone in China shot off the first rocket. History doesn't tell us who or why. It was probably a simple gadget, a small tube of wood or metal packed with gunpowder, carrying a clay or ceramic nose and a fuse for ignition. Originally, these early "skyrockets" were probably used in celebrations, much like our "fireworks" displays today.

Soon, though, using a long stick at the tail to help stabilize the rocket's flight, people began to devise less innocent purposes for the device. By 1050 A.D. they were mentioned frequently in military writings; the use of rockets against an enemy had begun.

The Spread of the Powder Rocket

The key to these early rockets' explosive power was the "black powder" packed tightly inside the narrow casing. The ingredients of this powder—charcoal, sulphur and saltpeter—had been known in China a long time before they were combined into the explosive mixture. The "recipe" quickly spread around the world. In England, Roger Bacon described it as early as the 1240s, and in Germany Albert Magnus wrote of its explosive potential. By 1429, France, intrigued then as now by the rocket's possibilities, had developed military rockets as part of its arsenal. By the 16th century many military strategists, weapons makers and inventors around Europe were studying and writing about the "rocket," while not actually putting their findings to use.

The picture began to change, however, in the 1790s when English troops took the brunt of extensive rocket barrages in India. That's when the English decided to include the weapons in their own military arsenal. Sometime around 1800 William Congreve, a colonel in the British army, set up the first English laboratory for rocket design and manufacture.

Under Congreve's direction small improvements in rocket design gave them greater efficiency. These new British rockets received their first major test during the War of 1812 when England used them against

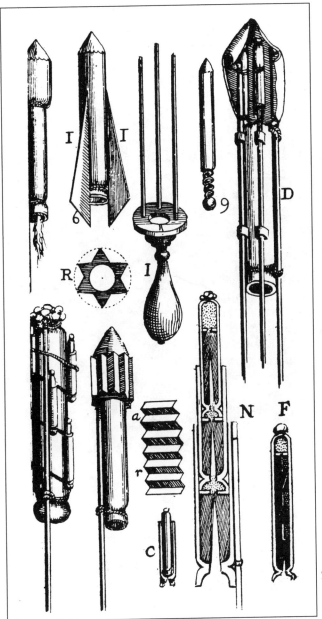

Early rocket designs from an 18th-century French Treatise

used occasionally by the American army during the Mexican War (between the U.S. and Mexico, 1846-48), and to a limited extent by both sides during the American Civil War, by the end of the century it had fallen into almost complete disfavor as a military weapon.

In the mid-1880s British rocket designer William Hale replaced the stabilizing stick of the Congreve rocket tail with metal vanes set at an angle inside the rocket's exhaust nozzle. The exhaust gas escaping past these vanes caused the rocket to spin, giving it better stability and accuracy.

Even these improvements didn't put the rocket back to work for the military, but it found some usefulness in 19th-century civilian life. Rockets sent up from onboard ships made effective signaling devices to announce the arrival, type and condition of cargoes. They were used ingeniously to shoot lifelines to stranded and sinking ships: passengers could attach themselves to the lines and be pulled or slide to safety. Some enterprising rocket enthusiasts even attempted to deliver mail by rockets over unbridged rivers and mountainous or rugged terrain.

Konstantin Tsiolkovsky Pioneers an Idea

Around the turn of the century, though, came the first glimmer of a more significant and inspired use for the rocket.

Seeing the rocket as a means of space travel was the inspiration of a Russian schoolteacher, Konstantin Eduardovitch Tsiolkovsky, born on September 17, 1857, in the province of Ryazan Gubernia, not far from Moscow.

Although later the military would once again take up the rocket as a weapon, hundreds of times more effective and deadly than ever before, Tsiolkovsky's new inspiration would change forever humanity's view of our place among the stars. It would allow, for the first time, the age-old dream of space travel to become a reality.

Tsiolkovsky, partially deaf from a childhood illness, was the son of a lumberjack who had emigrated from Poland. As a sickly and impoverished child he became an eager reader, finding comfort in whatever books he could find in his small village. It was a sparse harvest, however, and many of the books were old and out of date, but his father, described by Tsiolkovsky as an inventor-philosopher, encouraged the boy. Somehow, he educated himself with texts on math and physics, a little fiction and whatever he could

American troops, most significantly in the battle of Fort McHenry at Baltimore, Maryland. Although hardly yet "superweapons," the rockets had such dramatic effect that "the rockets' red glare" of that night still lives on in the U.S. national anthem, written by Francis Scott Key, a young American lawyer who witnessed the attack.

As a practical weapon of war though, the rocket still left much to be desired. Erratic and not very accurate, by mid-century it was replaced as a primary weapon by cannons, which were more powerful. Although

Soviet Rocket pioneer Konstantin Tsiolkovsky with his grandchildren

Sovfoto

find on astronomy. At 16, he went to Moscow, where he continued to educate himself in mathematics, physics and invention.

Three years later he returned to his hometown, where he tutored for a time before accepting a position teaching high school math and physics in Kaluga province—a job that allowed him to continue his reading and thinking, and one he would keep until his retirement in the 1920s.

"All my life," he later wrote, "consisted of meditation, calculations, and experimental work." At the age of 24 he submitted a scientific paper on the kinetic theory of gases (a theory describing the constant motion of minute particles of all matter) to the Society for Physics and Chemistry in St. Petersburg. The result was not exactly what the brilliant, self-taught young teacher had hoped for. Although impressed by the originality and discipline of Tsiolkovsky's thinking, the scientists at the Society were astounded to see that the young man was presenting solutions to problems that had already been solved 20 years before! Tsiolkovsky's books and resources were so out

of date and limited that he simply hadn't known that the solutions he had presented had already been found. Fortunately, although the situation was embarrassing, his readers at the Society recognized his capability and strongly encouraged him to continue his studies.

Like most early space pioneers, Tsiolkovsky had been an avid reader of Jules Verne's books in his youth. By the time he was 16 he had already begun his lifetime preoccupation with spaceships, rocket design and space travel. Like many others, he realized that if humanity ever wanted to travel beyond Earth, then we would have to find a realistic method of propulsion, or driving force, to escape the pull of Earth's gravity. Horse-drawn chariots, wishful thinking and friendly demons might be acceptable in novels and stories, but in the real world the laws of physics were not so forgiving.

Tsiolkovsky saw that the problem was really twofold. An enormous amount of power would be necessary for any object to escape from Earth and reach space. Once in space—to keep the object from becoming a "satellite" caught in the Earth's field of gravity—it had to have another means of propulsion that could operate in a near vacuum.

Tsiolkovsky's genius was not only to recognize that the only means of propulsion to do this job was a rocket, but also to outline his thinking in a manner that was at once logical, practical and visionary.

His reasoning was straightforward. In order to operate in space, maneuver, change direction, or add or reduce speed, some kind of force was needed. The force would have to be supplied by some kind of engine. On Earth, engines operate by converting heat into energy (the capacity to do work). The heat is created by combustion (rapid oxidation, or burning), and combustion requires oxygen. Since there was not enough oxygen in space to support combustion, the engine would somehow have to supply its own oxygen. Rockets, which provide their own oxygen as part of their fuel, could do that.

In his paper *Exploration of Space by Rocket Devices*, written in 1889 and published in 1903, Tsiolkovsky outlined his ideas for the use of rockets in space. This work became one of the most significant papers in the history of rockets and space travel.

Tsiolkovsky never actually built a single rocket, but from 1903 until his death in 1935, writing dozens of papers and articles from the isolation of his small house in Kaluga, he laid the basic theoretical foundations for future space flight. A true space visionary who saw in the future that humankind would not only travel in space but live and work in it, Tsiolkovsky also proposed other far-sighted ideas such as a space station that could be used for the launching of probes to be sent to explore other parts of the universe.

Through his insights into the principles of rocket technology and how rockets could be used to achieve space flight, K.E. Tsiolkovsky laid the groundwork for the modern space age.

What Is a Rocket?

What makes a rocket go? And what makes it so perfect for space travel?

If you've ever heard that "for every action there is an equal and opposite reaction," you're already familiar with the basic principle that accounts for a rocket's ability to move forward as it burns.

The principle, expressed in Newton's Third Law of Motion, is the same that enables a stream of water spurting out of a fire hose—or even from a garden hose at high pressure—to send you tumbling backward if you're trying to hold it steady. As the water spurts out in one direction, there's an equal and opposite reaction—a forceful push against the hose in the other direction.

A rocket is something like the hose in the example. Inside its motor, fuel is burned, producing very hot gases. The hotter a gas becomes, the faster and more energetically its molecules move in all directions. In a rocket these gas molecules have only one way to escape—out the open rocket tail or nozzle. The force of these gases streaming out of the rocket works like that of the water streaming out of the hose—it creates a forceful backward push, or reaction. Like the person holding the water hose, the rocket moves in the op-

posite direction. You can try this experiment in your own back yard.

The recoil of a gun when it's fired is another example of "rocket power" and Newton's law. So is the octopus's propulsion method—expelling water forcefully behind to speed itself forward.

Rockets differ from other powerful propulsion motors in one other important respect: they contain within them everything they need to work—both fuel and a substance, called an oxidizer, that can produce the oxygen the fuel requires to ignite and burn. The oxidizer is carried by the rocket either as part of the fuel itself or separately. This is the key reason for making use of rockets in the vacuum of space, where there is no air or oxygen for them to "breathe."

Jet engines, by contrast, are "air-breathing" engines, and so are automobile motors. Unlike rockets, they take oxygen from the air, combine it with the fuel they carry, ignite the combined mixture and propel themselves forward from the energy produced.

Rockets and rocket fuels differ widely, but they all have these two factors in common: The propulsion system is based on Newton's Third Law of Motion and the oxidizer is part of the package.

Robert Goddard, the "Rocket Man"

While Tsiolkovsky was working on his theories of rocketry and space travel, another visionary, thousands of miles away in the United States, was working independently, not only on theory, but on the actual building and testing of liquid-fuel rockets.

Robert H. Goddard was born in Worcester, Massachusetts, on October 5, 1882, almost 25 years after Tsiolkovsky. Like Tsiolkovsky's, Goddard's childhood was troubled with illness. As a youth he, too, had read Jules Verne and by the time he was 17 he had begun to wonder about the uppermost atmosphere of the Earth and had started to think about using rockets to investigate it.

By 1903, the same year Tsiolkovsky published *Exploration of Space* and the Wright Brothers made their historic flight at Kitty Hawk, Goddard was also already thinking about using rockets to travel to outer space. A typical New England "Yankee," a native of a region known for ingenuity and individuality, Goddard was a quiet, self-effacing young man with a love for tinkering and a practical turn of mind.

While studying physics at Worcester Polytechnic Institute and Clark University, he began experimenting with rockets and black powder. While working on his master's degree at Clark University he spent a few years researching electronics, but his love was always rocketry. After receiving his doctorate in 1911, he returned again to his rocket studies. The following year, at Princeton University, he showed how rockets could lift a light load of instruments high enough for serious atmospheric studies.

In 1914 Goddard received patents for a rocket nozzle and combustion chamber of his own design, and for a plan for a step or multistage rocket that he thought would be capable of space travel.

Up to that time, his experiments had been confined to the laboratory, but with the encouragement of Clark University, where he had returned as a physics instructor, he tried to finance field tests. Money, however, was tight, and he was forced, for the first of many times, to dip into his own small salary for funds.

Goddard began experimenting with ship-signaling rockets. They were small and not very powerful but they used black powder for fuel and were readily available. To increase the thermal efficiency of the small rockets, he also experimented with a new combustion chamber of steel, which he designed to adapt to different-sized nozzles, and he used "smokeless powder," more powerful than the black powder usually used.

Always the pragmatic thinker, Goddard wanted to *prove* the theory, held by some thinkers, that rocket engines did not have to push against anything to achieve thrust. It was a question important to space travel, since there is no air in space to push against. Theory was all fine and good, but Robert Goddard wanted to make a practical demonstration of it by way of actual "hands-on" experiments. First he placed a rocket combustion chamber inside a partial vacuum and fired it. No problem. Next he fired a pistol inside the vacuum and watched its recoil. Again, success. In each case the action resulted in an "equal and opposite reaction"—the thrust that actually propels a rocket. He had showed experimentally that a rocket really *would work* in the vacuum of space.

A small grant from the Smithsonian Institution came Goddard's way in 1916 allowing him to continue his experiments on controlled burning of solid rockets. World War I was in progress and in 1917 the Smithsonian urged the United States government to offer Goddard a separate grant to study possible uses of rockets in advanced weaponry. Moving to the Mount Wilson Observatory in Pasadena, California, the following year, Goddard briefly reintroduced the military application of rocketry. In the next months he designed and built a tube-launched recoilless missile, 18 inches long, 1 inch in diameter, propelled by a stick of nitroglycerin explosive. Something of a forerunner to the modern bazooka (a portable shoulder weapon that launches rockets), it was tested successfully, but the war ended before it ever went into production.

Back to his rocket studies, by 1919 Goddard submitted "A Method of Reaching Extreme Altitudes" to the Smithsonian. In this paper he outlined a plan for using rockets for meteorological research—a sound, practical idea, since meteorologists had already begun using balloons to measure wind, barometric pressure and temperature in the upper atmosphere.

At the end of his paper he dropped a verbal bombshell; for the first time he suggested his view that human beings might someday be able to reach space. He based this remarkable idea on three conclusions drawn from his experimental research: (1) a rocket could operate in a vacuum (beyond the Earth's atmosphere); (2) multistage rockets would be the best means for space travel; and (3) it was possible to reach the Earth's escape velocity (the speed needed to escape Earth's gravitational pull).

It was headline-making stuff—particularly Goddard's further suggestion that it would be possible to send a rocket to the Moon! Goddard, always practical, also proposed that the rocket could signal its

American rocket pioneer Robert Goddard in his New Mexico workshop

own arrival on the Moon's surface if it carried a payload of magnesium powder, which would flash on impact.

On January 1, 1920, *The New York Times* headlined:

BELIEVES ROCKET CAN REACH MOON.

Smithsonian Institution Tells of Professor Goddard's Invention to Explore Upper Air

Multiple Charge System

Instruments Could Go Up 200 Miles, and Bigger Rockets Might Land on Satellite

It was the first of many sensational headlines Goddard would make over the next few years, and it brought him his first taste of public ridicule.

Despite the Smithsonian's strong and embarrassed assertion that Goddard was *not* trying to reach the Moon, other news accounts referring to Goddard as "the Moon rocket man" hinted strongly that the whole enterprise was a crackpot operation.

Goddard was deeply unhappy at this sensationalized view of his work. As he confided woefully after one of his tests, "I'm not trying to hit the Moon. I'm just trying to get this one off the ground."

Goddard pressed on. He had begun to think about liquid-fuel rockets and had turned toward experimenting with different fuel combinations. Liquid fuel such as gasoline and liquid oxygen, he saw, had advantages over the solid fuels (like nitroglycerine or gunpowder) available then, including more even thrust and a higher exhaust velocity—the speed of gases expelled as the rocket fuel burns. By 1922 he had already built and tested a liquid-fuel motor.

In fact, other rocket pioneers had also begun to think along the same lines. Tsiolkovsky had proposed the use of liquid fuel in his writings, though few people outside the Soviet Union had read them. In 1923 the German pioneer Hermann Oberth published a widely read book, *Rocket into Interplanetary Space*, discussing the same possibility—an idea he had come to independently since Oberth had not yet read Tsiolkovsky's work and Goddard had not yet published his own test results. Goddard, already cautious by nature, became even more reticent after his experiences with the press, and throughout his career he was reluctant to share his results with others.

For the next few years Goddard continued his rocket and liquid-fuel experiments in Massachusetts, often to the complaints of his neighbors and the ridicule of skeptics. Finally, on March 16, 1926, at Auburn, with hard-won support from the Smithsonian Institution, he made the first successful firing of a liquid-fuel rocket.

On that clear, cold day, Robert Goddard turned on the liquid oxygen and gasoline valves of his rocket and lit the mixture with a blow torch. His wife, Esther, was on hand with her camera to document the exciting event, as the 10-foot (3m) long rocket took off. It flew a distance of 184 feet (56 m), reaching a height of 41 feet (12.5 m) at a speed of about 60 miles (96.6 km) an hour. The flight lasted only 2.5 seconds—but it flew.

With that brief, long-struggled-for rocket flight, Robert H. Goddard opened up a new era in the history of rocketry. Many years later. Dr. Eugene M. Emme of the National Aeronautics and Space Administration (NASA) called Goddard's achievement that day, "a feat as epochal in history as that of the Wright Brothers at Kitty Hawk." Over the next few years Goddard worked to refine and develop his new liquid-fuel rocket.

By July 17, 1929, he sent his first instrument payload aloft—including a barometer, a thermometer and a camera—fitted out with a parachute to bring them safely back to Earth. (A payload is any cargo or passengers carried by a rocket as part of its purpose or mission.) The instruments were recovered, though the parachute failed, and the flight caused so much noise and consternation that the police were called. The next day's headlines in *The New York Times* read:

METEOR-LIKE ROCKET STARTLES WORCESTER

CLARK PROFESSOR'S TEST OF NEW PROPELLENT TO EXPLORE AIR STRATA BRINGS POLICE TO SCENE

Shortly thereafter Goddard retreated to Roswell, New Mexico, where, financed by the Smithsonian and the Guggenheim Foundation, he could run his tests in the isolated desert, far from nervous neighbors.

Over the next few years, Goddard continued his research, focusing on gyroscopic control and stabilization (means of keeping a rocket upright), while he continued improvements on the fuel and cooling systems. In 1935 he fired a rocket that traveled faster than the speed of sound (1,086 feet, or 331 meters, per second) and another that reached 7,500 feet (2,286 m) in altitude.

On August 10, 1945, Robert H. Goddard died. At the time of his death he held 83 patents and applications for his work on rocketry, plus material for over 134 additional patents. They represented a lifetime of lone, persistent, patient designing and testing, redesigning and retesting. Throughout the late '30s and early '40s Goddard had single-handedly invented, developed or experimented with most of the techniques and ideas still incorporated in today's modern rockets. So great is the debt, in fact, that in 1960 the U.S. government issued a $1 million grant in Goddard's name, half to his estate and half to the Guggenheim Foundation, for the use of some 200 of his patents over the years. NASA's Goddard Space Flight Center in Greenbelt, Maryland, was named in his honor in 1959.

Ironically, though still neglected at his death by those whose support and recognition could have helped him most in the United States, Goddard's ideas on rockets and rocketry had already found their way to Europe. As the rumblings of World War II shook the world, the stage was set for the full power of the rocket to be realized—both as a deadly weapon of destruction and as the way to the stars.

3

WEAPONRY OR WIZARDRY?
THE GERMAN V-2 ROCKET

*Do you realize what we accomplished today?
Today the spaceship was born.*
—Walter Dornberger of the German Army
to Wernher von Braun after successful launch
of the A-4 rocket

The place was called Peenemünde. Located on an island in the Baltic Sea, it was the birthplace of a deadly weapon of war. Here, in the 1940s, under the skilled hands of a group of German engineers and scientists, the rocket came of age. In the grasp of the Nazi war machine its dark potential as a killing instrument was realized. Yet here, in the roar and flames of missiles carrying their messages of death and devastation, the door opened that would eventually take humanity into space.

Prelude of Innocence

The history of both Peenemünde and space began in 1927 when a group of German rocket enthusiasts formed the *Verein für Raumschiffahrt* (Society for Space Travel), which came to be known as the VfR. It was the first of a rash of amateur groups that formed around the world during this period, including the American Interplanetary Society (later the American Rocket Society) in 1930, the Soviet GIRD (Russian acronym for "Group for the Study of Reactive Propulsion") in 1931 and the British Interplanetary Society in 1933.

The German VfR had rallied around a young rocket theorist, Hermann Oberth, whose book *Rocket into*

Interplanetary Space, published in 1923, had stirred up considerable international interest. In it he had maintained that machines could be built that could fly beyond the Earth's atmosphere and escape Earth's gravity. What's more, he said, these machines could carry humans and their development and manufacture could be profitable, if conditions were right.

The youngest of the three great rocket pioneers, Oberth was 37 years younger than Tsiolkovsky and 12 years younger than Goddard. Born in 1894 in the Transylvanian Alps (at that time in Hungary, later absorbed into Romania), young Oberth had set off as a young man for the University of Munich to study medicine. His preference soon ran to courses in astronomy and mathematics. Like both Tsiolkovsky and Goddard, he was an independent thinker, a reader of Jules Verne and a visionary. Unfortunately, the three men did most of their early work completely unaware of each other.

The excitement of the newly formed VfR began to attract attention in Europe for the concepts of rocketry and space travel. While Goddard tried to play down the possibility of space travel and concentrated on scientific experimentation and rocket building, the German group surrounding Oberth was both more visionary and practical. One of their members, Max

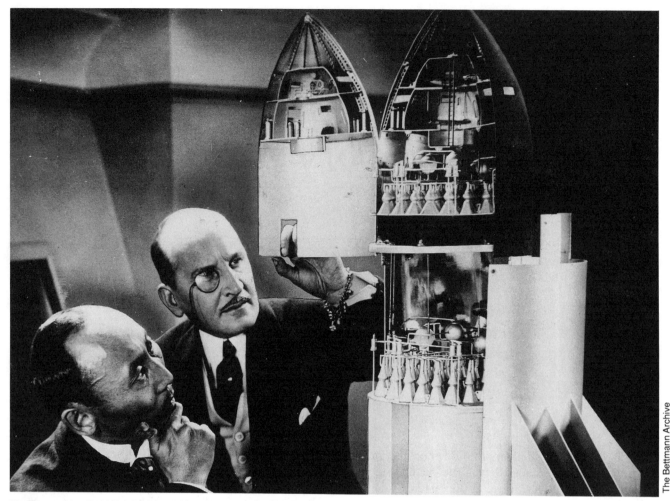

Hermann Oberth (right) inspects the rocket he built for the film *The Girl in the Moon*

The Bettmann Archive

Valier, teamed up with Fritz von Opel, the auto manufacturer, to build and test a flashy series of rocket-powered cars that caught the public imagination. Some members of the German Society frowned on this kind of publicity mongering. But by late 1929 the membership ranks swelled to about 900 members—including 19-year-old Wernher von Braun, who would figure prominently in rocket development both in Germany and, later, the United States.

In 1928, Oberth was hired as a consultant for rocket design on the set of German film director Fritz Lang's movie *The Girl in the Moon*. Because of the director's immense popularity, the gambit seemed certain to gain attention for the cause of rocketry and space flight, but Oberth also hoped he could spring the financing to build a real rocket in the process. Enthusiastic, Lang convinced the film company it would be a good publicity stunt and chipped in some funds himself. The film company agreed to the project, set

what turned out to be an impossible deadline and never came up with the money. Despite anguished, even frantic, attempts to meet the schedule, Oberth never got his rocket off the ground. Pumped-up advance notice of the rocket flight ended only in failure and keen embarrassment.

The year was not entirely black for Oberth and the German rocket buffs, however. A 5,000 franc prize for achievement in the new science of astronautics had been announced. The first prize, sponsored by the Astronomical Society of France, was awarded in 1929 to Hermann Oberth. In recognition of his major contribution, the donors doubled the prize money that year to 10,000 francs.

Aware by this time of some of Goddard's successes in the U.S., many of the core group in the VfR were eager to try their own hands at practical experimentation. Oberth, in fact, had given them a helpful start. His cone-shaped liquid-fuel motor named the

Kegeldüse (from *Kegel*, meaning cone), originally designed for the *Girl in the Moon* publicity fiasco, still remained half-manufactured. The VfR rounded up the parts, paid off the suppliers and put it together with Oberth's help. In 1930 the Kegeldüse was successfully tested and granted a certificate of performance.

Discouraged, however, by the bleak financial picture for rocket building, Oberth returned to his teaching position in Mediash, Romania, near his home town, where he would remain for several years. Meanwhile, the young VfR enthusiasts began building their own small liquid-fuel rocket using a smaller replica of Oberth's Kegeldüse combustion chamber. Donations from industry and members began to pour in, and they opened up a testing site, the Raketenflugplatz (rocket airfield), in an old World War I munitions dump just outside Berlin.

By May 1931, the VfR had successfully flown its first liquid-fuel rocket, the "Repulsor," designed by one of its members, Walter Riedel. That same spring two visitors, G. Edward Pendray and his wife, Lee Gregory Pendray, from their counterpart American Interplanetary Society, witnessed a static (nonmoving) rocket-motor test at Raketenflugplatz, watching with great interest and taking copious notes. On their return to the U.S., with new insights gained from the VfR on rocket design and liquid-fuel rockets the American group— previously strictly theoretical— would galvanize to begin building rockets of their own.

Meanwhile, with the VfR excitedly performing its tests outside Berlin, a more sinister future was developing for rocketry. By the provisions of the 1918 Treaty of Versailles, which was intended to prevent Germany from rearming after World War I, the German government was restricted from developing heavy artillery such as cannon and machine guns. Perhaps as an oversight, no mention had been made of rockets. The German army caught sight of this loophole as early as 1929 and by 1930 Germany had allotted $50,000 for development of new rocket weapons. Testing was set up at Kummersdorf outside Berlin and a young officer named Walter Dornberger was put in charge. The word went out that the army was interested in examining amateur rocket designs, since universities and industry appeared noticeably uninvolved and cool toward rocket development.

By the winter of 1931-32, a small, ranting madman and self-styled *führer* ("leader") Adolph Hitler, had become a major figure in German politics. The hardships of worldwide economic depression began to dry up the VfR's funding, and members dropped away as Germany's attention focused on the Nazi political machine and its objectives.

Hoping to attract military funding for their rockets, a small group of VfR members demonstrated a Repulsor rocket to army officials in 1932. A full-blown depression, however, and Hitler's takeover brought all private rocket research in Germany to an abrupt halt by 1933. Along with the several other amateur rocket groups that had sprung up in Germany, the VfR was dissolved—only six years after its founding. Within the 12 months from September 1930 to September 1931 alone, they had run nearly 300 static test firings and 87 actual rocket flights. Their influence had been felt worldwide, and they had given young rocket pioneers a place to try out their ideas.

They had also provided Nazi Germany with a ready-made pool of experienced rocket researchers—an asset the German military would not fail to notice.

The Birth of the German V-2

In late 1932, among those absorbed into Dornberger's eight-man army rocket development team was Wernher von Braun. Many other members of the VfR and the other amateur rocket groups were also eventually absorbed by the army project.

At Kummersdorf, Dornberger's group set to work. The VfR's most powerful rocket had been designed to produce a thrust (or push-off power) of 140 pounds— which it had never succeeded in doing. The army group, also working on liquid-fuel motors, tried instead for a hefty 650-lb. thrust, succeeding within just a few months. From there, they moved on to design a motor with an enormous 2,200-lb. thrust. At the same time they began designing the body of the rocket to be powered by the motors they were building. The project was dubbed the "Aggregate-1" or A-1 and, although the A-1 never flew, it was the first of the army's "A" series of rockets that ultimately would produce the A-4.

In 1934 two A-2s were successfully fired. The A-2's 25-foot length and 2-1/2-foot diameter were guided by three gyroscopes (devices to help keep the rocket upright during travel) and a few movable vanes in its exhaust stream (the stream of gases expelled from the burning fuel). At its best it went no farther than 7.5 miles high, landing only 7 miles (12 km) away. With the A-2, the army had not yet achieved its objectives, but a truly aimable ballistic missile was by now close at hand. It would be guided by the present mechanisms during the early part of its flight and then fall to Earth in a ballistic path, like a giant bullet.

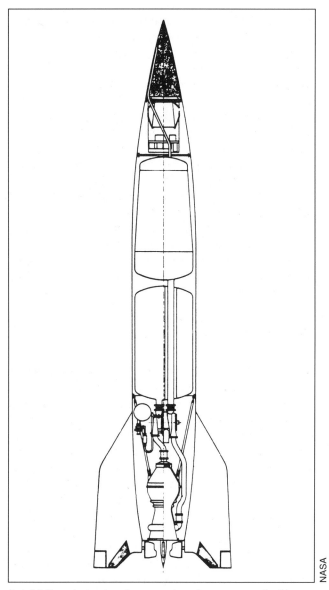

NASA

A-4 (V-2) rocket—deadly weapon and gateway to the Moon

It soon became clear that a new development and testing ground would be needed for Dornberger's program. In 1937 the Germany army-air force rocket experiment station was founded at Peenemünde, an isolated little town on an island jutting out into the Baltic Sea. Dornberger and von Braun were in charge of the team, by now swelled to 100 engineers and technicians.

Still focusing on liquid-fuel engines, the army team built the A-3, which had guidance problems, then proceeded to the A-5, which was successfully fired in 1938 and 1939.

On September 1, 1939, Germany invaded Poland and World War II began. Confident in their air force bombers, Hitler and the German government did not at first put much stock in the potential of rocket power, according to Dornberger's later accounts. However, the rocket team at Peenemünde continued to advance their expertise, and by 1941 they had begun work on the A-4, successfully testing it in 1942.

Now the A-4, along with the air force's low-flying pilotless winged bomb, caught the attention of Hitler and his advisors. By this time suffering from extensive pilot, crew and aircraft losses during bombing raids in England, the Germans gave both projects top priority.

Carrying more than a ton of explosive, the 46.2-foot A-4 could arc far up into the stratosphere, speed faster than sound across the English Channel and strike without warning at targets in London, about 350 miles (560 km) from the German shoreline. Peaceful city streets suddenly exploded into scenes of fiery destruction. The psychological terror caused by this thunderclap of instant death bore out German Minister of Propaganda Joseph Goebbels's new name for the A-4—the Vergeltungswaffen-2, or V-2, "vengeance" weapon.

From September 8, 1944, until March 27, 1945, when the attacks ended, 2,754 people were killed and 6,523 wounded in England by V-2s.

The governments of both the U.S. and the USSR recognized that the advanced technology of the V-2 had vast potential, for both advanced military rocketry and the future of space development and exploration.

By 1945, the Germans had begun to design an intercontinental ballistic missile (ICBM), designated the A-10, that would have had a range of 2,600 miles—10 times that of the V-2—and would have been capable of striking New York (which is why the missile was called "intercontinental"). It was to produce 440,000 pounds of thrust during the first stage, comparable to the thrust produced by the U.S. Titan 2 ICBM in 1961. Numerous other advanced rocket projects were on the drawing boards, putting the German army even more clearly on the cutting edge of rocketry design.

By then the war was drawing to a close. Defeats at the hands of the Soviet army at Stalingrad and the Americans and British in Africa in 1943 had greatly weakened German troop strength. By the time of the V-1 and V-2 strikes against London, the fighting was already getting closer to Germany. After massive U.S. bombing raids on Berlin, by March 25 all German troops had been driven back east of the Rhine River.

Caught at Peenemünde between advancing Soviet and American troops, von Braun and more than 100 of his group took a vote. Should they stay and stand

The Bettmann Archive

V-2 rocket being launched from Peenemünde in Germany during World War II

he and his men would know the location of. The crafty von Braun knew that this treasure and their own knowledge would ensure their safe conduct when the Germans surrendered.

On May 2, 1945, five days before the official German surrender, von Braun and his group turned themselves over to the American Army.

Of the principle V-2 scientists only one, Helmut Gröttrup, opted instead to go to the USSR. There, however, the Russians, who had seen their countryside ravaged by the Nazis, treated him like a captured war criminal and would allow him little freedom to work on their rocketry development in any major way. Managing to locate and confiscate some V-2 parts, the Soviets reconstructed the deadly rocket using their own engineers and scientists, firing their first V-2 on October 30, 1947.

Meanwhile, orders had come down from the U.S. joint chiefs of staff directing General Dwight D. Eisenhower to "preserve from destruction and take under your control records, plans, documents, papers, files and scientific, industrial and other information and data belonging to . . . German organizations engaged in military research." The secret and controversial plan, known as "Operation Paperclip," opened the American doorway to von Braun and his team.

The U.S. War Department authorized emigration of 127 German scientists and engineers to the United States. The first seven of the Peenemünde rocket team, headed by Wernher von Braun, arrived at Fort Strong, Massachusetts, under a veil of secrecy, on September 20, 1945. Additional members of the team and their families would come close behind them. Once arrived, they were offered government contracts and set to work. The U.S. Army wasted little time setting up its own rocket development project—and the V-2 experts from Peenemünde formed the nucleus.

Like a somewhat tarnished phoenix, the Space Age in America would be born from the bitter ashes of war.

their chances with the Soviets? Or go out in search of the Americans and surrender? They decided overwhelmingly that surrender to the Americans would probably be safer. Even though Germany had not yet surrendered, by the end of February the Germans had cleared out of Peenemünde, making their way south to join Dornberger and his group. In the process, von Braun had all of the V-2 technical documents hidden —creating a priceless cache of information that only

German Rocketry to 1945

1923 Publication of *Rocket into Interplanetary Space* by Hermann Oberth

1925 Publication of Walter Hohmann's *The Attainability of Celestial Bodies*, in which he discusses rocket motion in space

1927 July 5: Verein für Raumschiffahrt (Society for Space Travel, or VfR) is founded in Breslau, Germany (now Wroclaw, Poland). Early members include Johannes Winkler, Rudolf Nebel, Hermann Oberth, Walter Hohmann, Max Valier, Soviet Nikolai A. Rynin and French aviator Robert Esnault-Pelterie

1928 VfR publishes *The Possibility of Space Travel*, edited by Willy Ley. Contributors include Oberth, Valier and others

Max Valier begins experiments with rocket-powered cars, financed in part by Fritz von Opel

Oberth works on a rocket for publicity for Fritz Lang's movie *The Girl in the Moon*. But the rocket fails and the project is tabled.

1929 The VfR, by now about 900 members strong, recovers Oberth's unfinished rocket from unpaid suppliers in hope of finishing it.

Wernher von Braun, 19, becomes a member of the VfR

German army officials order its ballistics branch to undertake an investigation of the rocket's potentialities, with Walter Dornberger in charge

1930 **May 17:** Max Valier dies when a new liquid-fuel motor he has designed for one of his rocket cars explodes in a static test

VfR sets to work building its first liquid-fuel rocket, called Mirak, making use of Oberth's design for a combustion chamber, but it blows up in a static test.

The Reich Institute for Chemistry and Technology tests and certifies Oberth's rocket engine, the Kegeldüse

September 27: the VfR sets up a test site at an old World War I munitions storage area in Reinickendorf, a suburb of Berlin

1931 Mirak II, the sequel to the VfR's first rocket engine, blows up in the spring

February 21: Johannes Winkler, who has been working by himself in Dessau, 60 miles southwest of Berlin, succeeds in firing the first European liquid-fuel rocket

VfR plans for Mirak III and they begin to invite financial supporters to come to their tests. G. Edward Pendray and his wife, Lee Gregory Pendray, visit as official representatives of the American Rocket Society

Klaus Riedel and Willy Ley develop the "Repulsor," an alternate VfR design—a "metal egg" between two hollow tubes that act as fuel tanks. First test shoots about 60 feet. The second, May 14, goes about 200 feet

Repulsor II and Repulsor III follow. In August Repulsor IV goes more than 3,000 ft. (914.4 m) on its first test, its parachute opens, and it lands safely

The UFA Film Company sends a camera crew out to film a news reel about the group; crowds love the film

Financial resources for the VfR dry up as depression and Hitler's politics take their toll, but from September 1930 to September 1931 the VfR conducts nearly 300 motor test-stand runs and 87 actual rocket ascents

1932 July: Klaus Riedel, Rudolf Nebel and Wernher von Braun demonstrate a VfR rocket to German army officials

November 1: Wernher von Braun begins working on liquid-propellant rockets as a civilian employee of the German army under General Walter Dornberger

December: First liquid-fuel rocket motor tested at Kummersdorf explodes

1933 The VfR dissolves

Plans for "A"-series rockets begun at Kummersdorf, but the first A-1 tested explodes and development is abandoned

1934 **December:** Two A-2 rockets launched by von Braun and his colleagues from the island of Borkum in the North Sea. They reach altitudes of about 1.5 mi. (2.4 km)

1937 **April:** Peenemünde, on the North Sea, becomes the German army-air force rocket experiment station and Wernher von Braun's group moves in

December: First tests at Peenemünde are three A-3 rockets that all crash into the water after reaching an altitude of only a few hundred yards

1938 **Summer:** Successful tests of A-5 rockets

1939 **September 1:** Germany invades Poland and World War II begins

Autumn: Successful test of the A-5, which reaches a height of 5 miles and parachutes back down for reuse. A later test shows that it can tilt from the vertical, then continue on a curve out to sea. Recovery permits testing of internal mechanisms required for development of a larger rocket. Radio guide beams are also tested during this period

1941 Work begins on the A-4 rocket (later called V-2) at Peenemünde

1942 **August 17-18:** British Royal Air Force sends 600 bombers to raid Peenemünde, causing considerable damage and killing nearly 800

October 3: First successful A-4 launch

1943 Operational tests of V-2 rockets in Poland

1944 Spring: Underground assembly plant—called Mittlewerke—near the Harz Mountains produces 300 V-2 rockets a month (later, 900)

September 7: First V-2 attacks on London

1945 March: Last of the V-2s fired at England. Some 4,300 V-2s were fired, with 1,500 aimed at England, more than 1,100 of which landed there

May 2: Walter Dornberger, Werhner von Braun and others of the Peenemünde group surrender to the U.S. Army

May 5: Russian Army invades Peenemünde

September 20: "Project Paperclip" brings Werhner von Braun and other leading rocket experts to the U.S.

4

ADVANCING ON SPACE: ROCKET DEVELOPMENT 1945-1957

> *S*cience has reached such a stage that . . . the creation of an artificial satellite of the Earth is a real possibility.
>
> —A. N. Nesmeyanov,
> USSR Academy of Sciences,
> at the World Peace Council in Vienna, 1953

As World War II drew to a close in 1945, both Soviets and Americans had their eyes on the V-2 rocket builders. Knowing that the experience and skills of these men would make their own rocket-building program much easier, the Americans scooped the cream of the German rocket team. They also shipped home from Germany the components for 100 V-2 rockets and the priceless design and testing documentation from Peenemünde, but the Soviets didn't come up empty-handed. They walked off with a large group of secondary scientists and technicians, plus a considerable supply of V-2 parts. In both countries, the imported rocket technology and parts would mean thousands of hours of research saved, and ultimately would send humans into the far reaches of space far sooner than otherwise might have happened.

German Imports and Desert Tests in the U.S.

When Wernher von Braun arrived on American shores in 1945, for the most part rocket development in the United States had languished on the back burner during the 30 years since Goddard's first patent in 1914. Even on the back burner, though, the rocket research pot had still been simmering, and the beginnings of advanced research had developed, encouraged mostly by small amounts of private funding.

Work began in California at what would later become NASA's Jet Propulsion Laboratory. Here, scientists and engineers worked on rockets to be used to power airplanes as early as 1939. By December 1941, the first commercial rocket business in the U.S.—Reaction Motors, Inc.—was founded to build rocket engines for projects like the X-15 rocket plane (see chapter 6). Three months later another pioneer rocket company, Aerojet Corporation, was formed in California.

Meanwhile the military had shown little real interest. Finally in 1942, Robert Goddard, who had spent his life working virtually alone testing his rocket designs at his lab in Roswell, New Mexico, was swept up into government service. Uncle Sam set him to work on rocket packs to assist takeoff for heavy

JPL

A rocket test site at Arroyo Seco in 1941, near what is now NASA's Jet Propulsion Laboratory in Pasadena, California

aircraft at the U.S. Navy Bureau of Aeronautics in Annapolis, Maryland. The project was probably far more limited than he might have accomplished with stronger backing and vision, but the U.S. government still basically failed to see the bigger potentials of the work Goddard's genius had produced.

In the meantime the Army had established a Rocket Branch in 1943—but since the war was almost over, no crash program was begun. The work continued at a leisurely pace with the focus mainly on theory and jet-assisted aircraft.

Heading for the reaches of outer space was far from the minds of most military leaders as the war drew to a close, despite their rush to pick up V-2s and their makers. The idea of putting satellites in orbit was commonly considered possible, but the official position was that a satellite had no military use. Aside from groups like the American Rocket Society (and its cousin in England, the British Interplanetary Society), few nonmilitary objectives for entry into space were

on the minds of a nation recovering from the throes of war. And yet, today's expendable (unrecoverable) launch vehicles (ELV's) have developed directly from the sounding rockets and military missiles developed by the military between 1945 and 1957.

One Army-funded group called ORDCIT pursued upper-atmosphere research and began building rockets in May 1944. They launched a group of test rockets called Private A and Private F in December 1944 and April 1945 that would provide important groundwork for later developments. On the heels of that project the ORDCIT group launched another rocket for the Army, the WAC-Corporal sounding rocket (a rocket used for atmospheric tests, not as a weapon). Compared to the V-2, these rockets were all very small. The WAC-Corporal was only 16 ft. [4.8 m] long and 1 ft. [0.3 m] in diameter and could carry only light payloads (such as experimental instruments to explore the upper atmosphere). They did, however, soar as high as 20 miles (32 km).

By 1944, bigger rockets began to appeal to military leaders, although using rockets to soar into space did not. In November 1944, the U.S. Army signed a contract with General Electric Corporation to develop a rocket called Hermes, the first U.S. rocket to profit directly from the importation of Wernher von Braun and his German rocket team. A test site was set aside at White Sands, New Mexico, in February 1945, in the southwestern American desert where Goddard had discovered that the sky was clear, the weather relatively constant and the dangers to neighbors minimal. It was the same site where hundreds of scientists and engineers had labored in secret between 1942 and 1945 on a program, called the Manhattan Project, to develop the first nuclear bomb.

For the Hermes project about 300 railroad carloads of V-2 parts arrived by August 1945. Von Braun and his colleagues arrived in October. While the Hermes rocket itself never became important—the project eventually fizzled 10 years later for lack of Army interest—the testing done on it laid important groundwork for another powerful rocket, the Redstone, which would be a key player in the early American space program.

Although the White Sands work was underfinanced by a penny-pinching postwar military budget and was pretty boring to a team of men who were used to working on the cutting edge of rocketry, von Braun's crew set to work with great energy. When the budget provided only one metric wrench, they machined their own and they cannibalized axles so they could put wheels on the test stand for their rockets. By April 16, 1946, they made the first U.S. test of a V-2 rocket, and by December 1946 they had set a record height of 115 miles (185 km). Between 1946 and 1952 the U.S. tested 63 V-2s—primarily thanks to the expertise of the men they had imported from Germany.

It was during this period that a key ingredient for entering space began to take shape at White Sands— the development of multistage rocketry. By 1948 a program known as Project Bumper was developed to stack one rocket on top of another, using a V-2 and one of JPL's WAC-Corporals. Firing first and providing the initial lift-off, the V-2 would boost both into the sky and then drop away as the WAC-Corporal ignited to carry its load to greater heights than ever before. By February 1949, Project Bumper broke all records with a top speed of 5,250 mph (8,240 kh) and a peak altitude of 244 miles (400 km)—about the altitude of some U.S. Shuttle orbital flights today.

The Navy meanwhile began developing two more launchers—the sounding rockets Aerobee and Viking—for exploration of the upper atmosphere. For space exploration the Viking rocket, in particular, would provide the groundwork for the Navy's Vanguard rocket, which, next to the Army's Redstone rocket, would become the second key player in early U.S. space history.

But overall, the United States felt no pressure or urgency to develop rocket technology, and the work on rockets continued to move relatively slowly in the early postwar years.

U.S. Rocket Development Picks Up— Slowly

Progress continued to go slowly until 1949, when the USSR detonated its first nuclear device. Four years after the U.S. had shown its own nuclear power at Hiroshima and Nagasaki in its final days of war with Japan, Americans felt what the rest of the world had felt already: vulnerability to nuclear attack from a potentially unfriendly power. In reaction, attention to rockets was stepped up over the next 10 years throughout the U.S. armed forces.

In the little rural town of Huntsville in northern Alabama the Army established its new Redstone Arsenal in 1950. Here, where NASA's Marshall Spaceflight Center would later be located, the Army consolidated its rocket development effort and here they would build the Redstone rocket. That same year the entire German rocket team moved in from White Sands. Financing was still slow to come for their work, but for the first time the Germans began to have a chance to assimilate into an American community instead of being isolated in the desert.

In a rush to provide protective nuclear deterrence, Army and Air Force programs swung into high gear to develop the Atlas missile with the Titan as backup. Even though the U.S. and its allies had missile sites stationed in Europe within firing range of the Soviet Union, some U.S. military advisers saw a need for a weapon that could be launched from U.S. soil. The Atlas and the Titan would be intercontinental ballistic missiles (ICBMs) with this kind of long-distance power and accuracy. Soaring high above the clouds, an ICBM could be guided to a carefully positioned apex so that it would drop accurately, pulled to Earth ballistically by gravity like a bullet.

In the meantime, the Air Force would develop the Thor missile, an intermediate range ballistic missile (IRBM), which couldn't reach quite as far—only 1,500 miles (2,400 km)—but would fill in until the ICBMs were ready. The Thor missile program received its go-ahead in September 1955.

Launch of the first Bumper missile from Cape Canaveral, July 24, 1950

From these same military programs the U.S. would develop— as the Soviets would as well—the power to send objects, and, ultimately, human beings into space. As early as 1954, the Office of Naval Research asked von Braun if he knew a way to send a small scientific satellite into orbit by combining existing rockets.

Von Braun—whose enthusiasm for space dated back to his early membership in the German rocket society,

the VfR—strongly maintained that the answer was yes. The Redstone missile he and his colleagues at Redstone Arsenal had been working on, he said, had enough power to launch clusters of small, solid-fuel rockets such as those already developed for military defense. Together, the combined rocket power could send a small 5-to-7-pound satellite into orbit. The Army gave his team cautious approval to work on the satellite-launching project if it didn't slow down the development of the Redstone itself.

Meanwhile, scientists and government leaders worldwide were working on an international scientific event called the International Geophysical Year, due to begin July 1, 1957. Wouldn't it be exciting, the international committee for the IGY put forth, if participating nations would try to orbit a satellite in celebration?

In the U.S., internal dissension—not cooperation— was the name of the game. The Army had its Redstone rocket; the Air Force wanted to launch an ambitiously heavy satellite with its Atlas ICBM, which was still in development; and the Naval Research Laboratories wanted to build a new rocket, called Vanguard, for the purpose. Studies were made; debates were held; proposals and counter proposals were put forth.

In the end, President Dwight Eisenhower made a decision. The U.S. would support the Vanguard project for the IGY event. (Atlas wasn't really far enough along to be in the running, and Redstone didn't "look good" because of its military history.)

In fact, though, von Braun and his Redstone team were so close to the goal, that the Army sent inspectors to his subsequent test firings to make sure he wouldn't "accidentally" send a satellite into orbit and upstage the Vanguard.

Meanwhile, on the Soviet Side . . .

Even more than the Americans, the Russians had been preoccupied by war in the years up to 1945, and before that, by revolution and internal strife. As a result rockets were not front and center stage for them, either, but ever since the time of Tsiolkovsky, Russians had been dreaming of rocketry and space.

N.I. Tikhomirov had begun practical experiments with powder rockets in the 1890s and began campaigning for government funding with a letter to Lenin as early as 1919. With the blessing of the Revolutionary Military Council, Russia's first research laboratory for studying solid-fuel rockets was founded in March 1921 by Tikhomirov and his colleague, Vladimir Artmeyev.

Sovfoto

Soviet rocket designer Sergei Korolev in 1946. Although a political prisoner for many years, working in anonymity for most of his life, Korolev would become a key figure in the USSR's future successes in space exploration

A swell of active interest had developed in the '20s. F.A. Tsander had submitted his spaceship design for interplanetary travel to the Moscow Conference of Inventors in 1921. By 1924 Tsander's fertile imagination had come up with the novel idea that a rocket plane could speed beyond the atmosphere and continue its flight using its wings—no longer needed in airless space—for fuel.

That same year saw the founding of the Society for the Study of Interplanetary Travel with almost 200 members, including Tsiolkovsky and Tsander. The Association of Inventors put on an exhibition of space vehicle design in 1927 that included the works of Tsiolkovsky, Oberth and Goddard. A monumental three-volume encyclopedia of rocketry and space flight, published in 1928, created an international stir for its thoroughness and ambition.

During this period Tikhomirov's solid-fuel rocket lab moved to Leningrad and in 1928 was renamed the Gas Dynamics Laboratory or GDL, reporting to the Military Research Council. It would become the seat of much important Soviet rocket research, especially

focusing during this period on short-range field rockets that could be used by Army troops.

By 1929, the Soviet emphasis, like Goddard's and the Germans', began to shift from solid-fuel to liquid-fuel propellants. After the death of Tikhomirov at age 70 in 1930, the GDL began to grow rapidly, soon dividing into seven different subgroups—five of them in various areas of research, but for the first time the GDL had subgroups concentrating on production and procurement as well. The lab began work on its first liquid-propellant rocket, the ORM-1, in 1930, followed shortly by the ORM-2.

By this time the popular and professional swell of interest in rockets had reached such proportions in the Soviet Union that several groups were founded for the study of reactive propulsion, or rocketry, and in April 1932, Sergei P. Korolev stepped up as head of design at the first experimental Soviet rocket design center in Moscow. Just 29 years later he would see his spacecraft design take the first human being into space—but there was still a lot of ground to cover before that day would come!

In 1937, Soviet rocket development was dealt a severe blow when a purge under Communist leader Josef Stalin sent Korolev to a Siberian labor camp for "treason." Years of imprisonment followed for Korolev, as well as many of his colleagues. Although the Soviets soon began to draw again on Korolev's talents during this period, the public record of his existence ended until the 1950s. Even then, until his death, he was officially referred to in the press only as the anonymous "chief designer" of the Soviet space program, not by name.

From Peenemünde to the Steppes

During WWII, the Soviets had succeeded in developing a flying bomb, Project 212, which resembled the German V-1. Additionally, they developed a rocket-powered glider, the RP-318-I, designed by Korolev and flown for the first time in 1940. Unlike an airplane, it was towed into the air and then powered by a rocket during flight.

For the Soviets, as for the Americans, peace brought access to German technology, but the Soviets did not give their imported German rocket specialists the same kind of important positions the Americans had given von Braun and his men. They had a lot of good reasons for treating the Germans differently than the Americans did: they had felt Hitler's attacks directly on their homeland—they probably trusted the Germans less—and, except for Helmut Gröttrup, the German personnel they recruited were not of the same caliber as those recruited by the Americans.

In any case, Gröttrup had returned to Germany by 1953, along with most of the rest of his colleagues. The remainder stayed no more than five years longer. In general, the Soviets had never trusted them, had isolated them from their own engineers, and had limited any exchange between the two groups.

Nonetheless the Russians picked up considerable technology from the V-2 tests and the Germans. They also learned German engineering and managerial techniques and soon began to etch a formidable history of their own in the annals of rocketry.

And the Race Was On

With the Soviet nuclear detonation in 1949 tensions increased between the U.S., along with its European allies, and the Soviet Union. The Cold War, a period of animosity short of actual war between the Soviet Union and the U.S., blew frostily. An official Soviet "Iron Curtain" policy cut off communication between the U.S. and the Communist countries allied with the USSR, creating a political atmosphere of hostility and mistrust.

Up to this point, rocketry had not really attracted governmental attention in the U.S., and for the most part Americans were unaware of the legacy of Soviet technical expertise dating from the pre-war days. As a result, on September 17, 1957, when the Soviets announced they would shortly send a satellite orbiting around the Earth in celebration of the International Geophysical Year, the reaction in the U.S. was disbelief. Surely the Soviets were bluffing!

However, 17 days later, on October 4, 1957, a new blinking object high overhead in the night sky became visible even to the most skeptical eye. It told the tale clearly enough: The USSR had launched Sputnik 1, the world's first artificial satellite. As Americans watched incredulously, the 184-pound (83-kg) ball orbited the Earth twinkling and beeping. It was small and unimpressive by today's standards, but it was giant in its impact. Sputnik and the Soviets had changed humankind's perception of the universe forever.

U.S. Rocketry to 1957

1903 First airplane flight by Wright Brothers at Kitty Hawk, North Carolina

1914 Robert Goddard is granted U.S. patent for multistage rocket

World War I begins

1916 Goddard receives grant from Smithsonian Institution for rocket development

1917 U.S. enters war in April

1918 World War I ends

1919 Goddard publishes "A Method of Reaching Extreme Altitudes," a report that asserts the feasibility of exploring the Moon

1926 **March 16:** Goddard runs test flight of the first liquid-propellant rocket

1930 **March 21:** American Interplanetary Society founded

1931 The Pendrays (founding members of the AIS) travel to Germany, visit German Rocket Society (VfR) and return with copious notes on rocket design

1932 AIS does stationary successful test of its own first rocket (liquid-fuel) in November, but due to a later accident it never flies

1933 **May 14:** AIS runs successful rocket test on Staten Island

1934 American Interplanetary Society changes its name to American Rocket Society

September 9: ARS successfully flight tests liquid-fueled rocket

1935 Goddard launches a gyroscopically stabilized rocket that flies faster than sound

Goddard publishes "Liquid Propellant Rocket Development"

1936 GALCIT (Guggenheim Aeronautical Laboratory at California Institute of Technology) is founded at what is now the Jet Propulsion Laboratory (JPL)

1939 Caltech program to develop high-velocity aircraft rockets (HVARs) is begun

One of Goddard's patents is published in translation in *Flugsport*, a semi-popular German aviation magazine

World War II begins

1940-41 Concerted rocket development in U.S. (military)

1941 U.S. enters the war

Reaction Motors Inc. founded by key ARS members

First JATO flight of a light plane in U.S.

1942 Army Col. L. Skinner develops bazooka for use in combat

1944 June 22: U.S. Army awards contract to California Institute of Technology to research and develop long-range rockets

1945 May 2: Wernher von Braun and more than 100 of the German Peenemünde rocket team turn themselves over to U.S. Army

May 7: War ends in Europe with German surrender

August 10: Robert Goddard dies

September 20: "Operation Paperclip" brings von Braun and his Peenemünde colleagues to U.S., and by October they begin work at White Sands Proving Grounds, New Mexico

September 26: JPL launches the WAC-Corporal, a rocket specifically designed for upper atmosphere research

1946 April 16: First U.S. V-2 firing, at White Sands

June 28: Naval Research Laboratory sends V-2 rocket to 62 miles (99.8 km) altitude for upper air research

1947 May 22: First radar ground control system used in launch of Corporal E surface-to-surface missile at White Sands

June 20: "Bumper Project" initiated by Army

September 6: V-2 rocket launched from the U.S.S. *Midway* aircraft carrier

October 14: Charles E. Yeager breaks "the sound barrier" in X-1 rocket-powered plane

1949 February 24: Two-stage V-2/WAC-Corporal (Project Bumper) launched from White Sands attains record height of 244 miles (393 km)

May 3: First test of the Viking rocket (the basis for the Vanguard rocket), reaching an altitude of 51 miles (82 km)

1951 August: Record altitude for single-stage rocket of 135 miles (217 km) achieved in Viking 7 rocket test

1952 March 22: In an article in *Colliers* magazine Wernher von Braun proposes a spinning wheel-shaped space station

1955 July 15: President Dwight D. Eisenhower announces decision to launch a scientific satellite

September 9: Project Vanguard given go-ahead for first satellite launch in favor of the Project Orbiter Redstone rocket

1956 September 20: Suborbital launch of three-stage Jupiter C rocket (based on Redstone rocket) from Cape Canaveral carries 86.5-pound (39.2 kg) payload to an altitude of 680 miles (1,094 km). But government is going with the Vanguard rocket for satellite launch

1957 October 4: Soviets launch world's first artificial satellite, Sputnik 1

Soviet Rocketry to 1957

1894-1897 First practical rocket research in Russia—N.I. Tikhomirov builds powder rockets and performs experiments

1915 Y.I. Perelman's book *Interplanetary Travel*, in which he concludes that of all the science-fiction methods of space travel the rocket is the only realistic means, is published in Russia

1917 Russian Revolution

Valentin Petrovitch Glushko begins studies of applications of reactive motors to space flight

1919 Tikhomirov writes to Lenin about his solid propellant rocket. But approval for government funding does not come for another two years

Yuri Vasilyevich Kondratyuk finishes first stage of his analysis of basic principles of rocket propulsion

1921   The first research laboratory for the study of solid-fuel rockets in Russia is founded in March by Tikhomirov and Vladimir Artmeyev, on approval from the Revolutionary Military Council

After 14 years of study, F.A. Tsander submits his proposal to the Moscow Conference of Inventors for his design of a spaceship for human interplanetary travel

V.P. Vetchinkin began studies into using rockets for travel into space. He made lecture tours around the country up through 1925

1923   Glushko corresponds with Tsiolkovsky about technical aspects of Glushko's work

1924   Tsander developed an idea for a rocket plane—fueled, once out of the atmosphere, by its own wings, which it would no longer need

In April G.M. Kramarov was head of an Interplanetary Travel section of the Military Research Society of the Air Force Academy—which a few months later became the Society for the Study of Interplanetary Travel, with nearly 200 members, including Tsiolkovsky, Tsander and Vetchinkin

1925   Tikhomirov's lab moves to Leningrad

D. A. Grave starts a space study society in Kiev that contributes to an exhibition on June 19 with lots of publicity and lectures. Enthusiasm in the USSR is now high and many local societies or local branches are formed

1927   In April and June an exhibition by the Association of Inventors features space vehicle design, especially spaceships and space rockets, covering the work of rocket research greats like Tsiolkovsky, Oberth, Goddard, Valier and Esnault-Pelterie

1928   Tikhomirov's lab becomes the GDL or Gas Dynamics Laboratory, responsible to the Military Research Council. The Soviets show much interest in applying principles of rocketry to military purposes—especially short-range field rockets for use by troops

N.A. Rynin begins publishing his three-volume encyclopedia of rocketry and space flight

1929   Kondratyuk publishes extensive book on rocket theory

Glushko proposes to the government a more focused concentration on liquid-propellant rockets. Also proposes an electric rocket (operated with a beam of electrons). By 15 May Glushko joins the GDL as head of the department to work on liquid propulsion

1930   Tikhomirov dies at 70. B.S. Petropavlovsky becomes head of the GDL, initially a research-oriented organization that becomes more applied over the next few years

By 1930 work begins on ORM-1, a liquid propellant rocket motor, followed in a few months by work on ORM-2

1931   GIRD (Group for the Study of Reactive Propulsion—the acronym is from the Russian) is founded in Moscow (headed by T.F. Tsander) and in Leningrad (started by V.V. Raxumov). With this group begins the practical development of both rockets and jet planes in the USSR. Perelman and Rynin are active in Len-GIRD; Korolev an important figure in Mos-GIRD. Other major cities form their own groups

USSR's first real rocket engine—the ORM-1 experimental reaction engine—is built and tested by the GDL

By this time the GDL is working on booster rockets to assist aircraft into the air (JATO), construction and test of solid propellant rocket projectiles and design and assembly of the first Soviet liquid propellant rocket motors

1932   By this time other organizations have been formed to apply the GDL's laboratory concepts to actual flight tests

In April, 29 years before Gagarin's flight, Korolev is put in charge of the first experimental Soviet rocket design center in Moscow; it embraces various existing organizations

1933   A new organization in December establishes that all research be coordinated in the RNII (Rocket-science Research Institute—the acronym is from the Russian). Kleienov is director and Korolev co-director

1937   Stalin purge sends rocket designer Korolev to a labor camp, where he is imprisoned

1939   First flight of the Soviet flying bomb, Project 212, similar to the German V-1—catapulted into the air by a powder rocket on a sled

1940   First flight of the RP-318-I rocket-powered glider designed by Korolev

1945   **May 5:** Soviet troops arrive at the abandoned Peenemünde rocket development center

By May 16, of the German rocket team Helmut Gröttrup alone decides to cast his lot with the Soviets. But by 1945 the Russians have been moving for 24 years in the same direction as Germany toward rocket development—in theory if not in practice

1945-46 First test trials of Soviet version of German V-2 made by GDL-OKB

1946 Soviets reorganize rocket production at Peenemünde

July-August: S.P. Korolev designs "stretched" V-2

October 28: Soviet recruits from among the German rocket engineers arrive in Moscow

1947 October 30: Launch tests begin of Soviet V-2 type missiles

1951 March 21: German rocket experts recruited to USSR begin to return to Germany. All will return by November 28, 1953

1954 GDL-OKB begins to develop engines for first Soviet ICBM

1955 May 26: Launch of two dogs into suborbital flight. The Soviets conduct seven more such experiments between 1955 and 1957

May 31: Construction begins on the Baikonur Cosmodrome launch site (actually located near Tyuratam) on the steppes of Kazakhstan

5

SPUTNIK AND EXPLORER 1
BEGIN THE SPACE AGE:
1957-1960

*A*ll right. Let's get on with it!
—T. Keith Glennan,
first NASA administrator, regarding
development of the space program,
October 7, 1958

The tiny aluminum capsule called Sputnik 1 revolutionized not only the way humankind saw the universe, but also the way Americans saw themselves. The people that prided itself on "Yankee ingenuity" had forcibly been one-upped by the Soviets that crisp October morning in 1957. The space age had dawned, leaving Americans behind in the dark.

Sputnik's 23-inch (58.4-cm) sphere was hardly bigger than a beach ball, yet its aluminum skin twinkled in the night sky for all to see. Its four metal antennae stretched out 96 to 116 inches (244 to 295 cm) to send radio signals beaming down as it orbited the Earth. Their "beep-beep" sound over the next 21 days recounted its onboard temperature and seemed like a heartbeat coming from beyond the safe envelope of Earth's atmosphere.

Just in case anyone imagined that *Sputnik 1* was a fluke, the Soviets followed up less than a month later with another launch on November 3. *Sputnik 2*, weighing a hefty 1,121 pounds (508.5 kg),

demonstrated to the world that the Soviets had rocket power far greater than the United States (with its 3-pound and 31- pound (1.4 kg and 14 kg) satellites readying for launch).

In addition, *Sputnik 2*'s cargo showed that the Soviets were already serious about sending, not just objects but, ultimately, *people* into space. For on board *Sputnik 2* flew a small dog named "Laika," the first living creature to orbit beyond Earth's atmosphere in the weightlessness and vacuum of space.

Laika (whose name means Barker in Russian) was supplied with food and oxygen and wired to relay biological information back to Earth, providing the first clues anyone had about what effects space travel would have on living things. For 10 days she survived in space—proof that living organisms could endure there. Laika died, however, even before the oxygen ran out and in any case the Soviets had made no provision for recovering her capsule. She gave her life for the benefit of the humans that would follow.

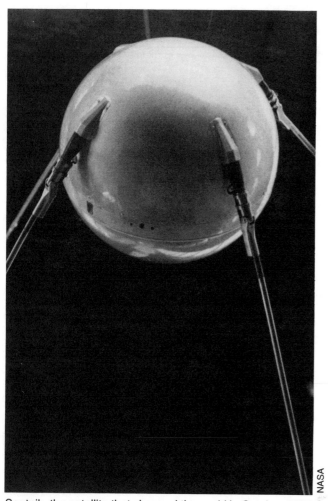

NASA

Sputnik, the satellite that changed the world in October 1957

Army and Navy Scramble to Catch Up

Meanwhile, the U.S. tried desperately to catch up and recover face. The Soviets now had a definite edge, and the eyes of the world watched expectantly.

Project Vanguard—the officially adopted plan begun by the Naval Research Laboratory in 1955 to lob a satellite into orbit using a Vanguard rocket—hovered close to completion. A better-late-than-never recoup seemed within reach. On December 6, 1957, at Cape Canaveral, a Vanguard rocket ignited on schedule as the countdown finished, but seconds later, the first U.S. attempt to launch a tiny 6-inch (15-cm) satellite exploded in a huge ball of fire.

By now the U.S. government had hedged its bets on Vanguard. As early as November 8, following the Sputnik 1 and 2 launches, President Eisenhower had finally told the Army to ready an alternate to the Navy's program. Since Wernher von Braun's rocket

team had been waiting in the wings for such an opportunity, it took them only 84 days to gear up their missile program for the new space age. They quickly modified their Jupiter C four-stage rocket (essentially a slightly lengthened Redstone missile), which they called Juno 1. Meanwhile, the Jet Propulsion Laboratory (JPL) at the California Institute of Technology built a small satellite called Explorer 1, which would carry a load of scientific experiments designed by James Van Allen of the University of Iowa. On January 31, 1958, Juno 1 lifted off the launch pad at Cape Canaveral, and Explorer 1 veered into space to become the first U.S. satellite to orbit the Earth.

Just under 7 feet (205 cm) long and 6.5 inches (16.5 cm) in diameter, the 31-pound (14 kg) satellite seemed a bit puny compared to the two Sputniks, but cutting a higher orbit, Explorer 1 set out to study cosmic rays, micrometeorites and temperatures at altitudes up to 1,583 miles (2,548 km) as it beeped home its data via two tiny transmitters. In the process, it confirmed the existence of a belt of radiation trapped between 620 to 3,000 miles (1,000 to 5,000 km) above the equator—one of two such regions now known as the Van Allen Belts, named after the man responsible for their discovery.

On the heels of the Explorer victory, however, came yet another disappointment for the U.S. as the second Vanguard effort broke up in flight in February 1958. Termed "Kaputnik" and "Flopnik" by the British press, the two Vanguard disasters somewhat soured the sweet smell of success, and an attempted launch of Explorer 2 in early March likewise fizzled. But at last, in March 1958, Vanguard 1 soared into space.

Sporting a radio transmitter that would still be sending data nearly six years later, Vanguard 1 proved reliable and sophisticated in electronics and engineering, despite its tiny 3-pound (1.4 kg) weight amounting to less than one sixtieth Sputnik 1's. Precise data obtained from tracking the Vanguard 1 radio signal led geophysicists for the first time to recognize the pear-shaped form of the Earth (narrow at the North Pole).

Not resting on their laurels, the Soviets followed up with yet another impressive launch—the 2,926-pound (1,327-kg) Sputnik 3. This much heftier and bigger satellite was launched May 15, 1958, and measured the pressure and composition of the upper atmosphere, the number of micrometeoroids, and solar and cosmic radiation (rays of energy from the sun and other bodies in the universe).

By now the U.S., as well as the USSR, had its eyes riveted on space. Congress increased funding for the National Science Foundation by 300 percent in 1958.

Government studies and special offices abounded, including the President's Science Advisory Committee and the Senate Preparedness Subcommittee (chaired by Senator Lyndon B. Johnson), both of which concluded that the U.S. should take a bold, strong stance in space technology.

On July 29, 1958, President Eisenhower signed the National Aeronautics and Space Act of 1958, which terminated the existing National Advisory Committee for Aeronautics (NACA) and formed a National Aeronautics and Space Administration (NASA). On October 1, 1958, NASA was officially established. The new civilian space agency reflected Eisenhower's commitment to projecting an image at home and abroad that "outer space be devoted to peaceful and scientific purposes." While military involvement in space continues to be high, this commitment to civilian space development is a premise that still holds powerful attraction to many U.S. space advocates today.

Just a week later NASA approved Project Mercury—a bold, visionary plan "to send a man into orbit, investigate his capabilities and reactions in space, and return him safely to Earth." NASA absorbed many of the talents that had helped bring about the space age—including all 8,000 employees of NACA. The Army's Jet Propulsion Laboratory came under NASA jurisdiction in December, and by July 1960 the Redstone Arsenal became NASA's George C. Marshall Space Flight Center, with Wernher von Braun in charge.

Meanwhile, both the U.S. and the Soviets would spend the coming two-and-a-half years learning how to use space and preparing for the moment when humans might venture there.

Learning to Make Use of Space

Today television relays by satellite, Landsat (earth observation satellite) images, weather forecasting based on satellite images and hundreds of other satellite applications seem commonplace. According to a December 1977 edition of the Soviet newspaper *Pravda*, however, two years before Sputnik, many reputable Soviet scientists couldn't think of any uses for artificial satellites. The same was no doubt true in the United States.

Yet, once the technology had been proven, efforts—both successes and failures—snowballed rapidly. Between December 1957 and September 1959, when Vanguard 3 was successfully launched, the U.S. made 11 attempts to launch Vanguard satellites, with only three successes. The year 1958 saw a 50 percent

Official U.S. Navy Photograph

Although this October 1957 Vanguard test got off the ground, the next one (which was meant to carry the first U.S. satellite into orbit) collapsed on the launch pad

failure rate in attempted launches in the U.S. and the Soviet Union combined. Yet both nations pressed on.

By Christmas 1958 the world had heard the first broadcast of the human voice from space. Launched December 18 atop an Atlas booster, the Project Score satellite transmitted the recorded voice of President Eisenhower.

The U.S. Air Force followed up with a series of satellites called Discoverer—the first going into orbit on February 28, 1959—to conduct various kinds of space research, including communications and photographic missions.

In August 1959, Explorer 6 spun out 16,373 miles (26,344 km) above the Earth's surface to take the first television pictures of our planet. For the first time we caught a glimpse of what Earth looked like from the outside looking in. The first weather satellite, TIROS

1, was not far behind, sending 22,952 photos back to Earth from April 1 to June 17, 1960.

That same summer a revolution in communications was launched with Echo 1, an enormous, 100-foot (30.5-m) aluminum-coated high-tensile polyester balloon lobbed into Earth orbit from Cape Canaveral and then inflated in space. From there it acted as a communications satellite, passively relaying voice and TV signals bounced off it by two ground stations. Within a week Bell Telephone Laboratories had completed the first transatlantic wireless transmission, between New Jersey and France, bounced off Echo 1.

The year 1960 also brought several other firsts: the first navigation satellite (Transit 1B) to reach orbit, although too low for ships to calculate their positions by as intended; the first experimental infrared surveillance or "spy" satellite (Midas 2); and a communications satellite (Courier 1B) that recorded signals and repeated them on command. Many more would follow rapidly in the years to come.

Milestones in Space—The Sputnik Era, 1957-1960

1957   August: First Soviet intercontinental ballistic missile (called "Sapwood" by NATO) is launched

October 4: The space age begins with the Soviet Union's launch of Sputnik 1, the world's first artificial satellite

November 3: The Soviets launch Sputnik 2, the world's second artificial satellite, carrying the dog Laika

December 6: Vanguard, meant to carry the first U.S. artificial satellite, explodes seconds after firing on the launch pad.

1958   January 31: The U.S. launches Explorer 1, the first successful U.S. Earth satellite, fired into orbit atop a Jupiter-C (Redstone) launch vehicle called Juno 1

February 5: Second Vanguard launch failure

March 5: U.S. attempt to launch Explorer 2 satellite fails

March 17: U.S. makes the first successful Vanguard launch of an artificial satellite

March 26: U.S. Explorer 3 satellite launches atop a Juno 1 (Jupiter C) booster

May 15: Soviets launch Sputnik 3, weighing in at a hefty 2,926 lbs. (1,327 kg), about 45 times the weight of the three American satellites combined

July 26: U.S. launches Explorer 4 atop a Juno 1 booster

July 29: National Aeronautics and Space Administration (NASA) founded in U.S.

October 1: NASA officially goes into operation

October 7: NASA announces the beginning of Project Mercury—a plan to send a human into orbit

October 11: U.S. launches Pioneer 1, which ascends to an altitude of 70,717 miles (113,780 km)

November 8: U.S. Pioneer 2 suffers a launch failure

December 6: U.S. launches Pioneer 3, reaching an altitude of 63,580 miles (102,300 km)

December 18: U.S. launches the weighty 8,750-lb. (3,969-kg) Score satellite atop an Atlas launcher

1959   January 2: USSR launches Luna 1, intended to impact the Moon, which instead flies by at a distance of 3,728 miles (5,955 km) and becomes the first spacecraft to orbit the Sun

February 17: U.S. successfully launches Vanguard 2

February 28: U.S. Air Force launches first Discoverer satellite

March 3: Pioneer 4 is launched to become the first U.S. lunar flyby, at a distance of 37,300 miles (60,000 km)

April 2: NASA announces the names of the "Mercury Seven," the first U.S. astronaut team

May 28: U.S. recovers two monkeys, Able and Baker, after launch in Jupiter nosecone from Cape Canaveral. Able later dies, however

September 12: The Soviets' Luna 2 impacts the Moon

October 7: USSR's Luna 3 (launched October 4) takes the first look at the far side of the Moon, sending back the first images ever taken of the side we never see from Earth

November 26: U.S. lunar probe Atlas Able 4 suffers a launch failure

1960   April 1: U.S. launches TIROS 1, the first successful meteorological satellite, for three months observing Earth's weather from space

April 13: U.S. launches the first experimental navigation satellite, Transit 1B

May 24: Midas 2, the first experimental infrared surveillance satellite launched by U.S.

August 12: U.S. launches Echo 1, a giant aluminized balloon, into orbit to become the first passive communications satellite

August 19-20: First return of a living creature from orbital flight in space: Soviets launch and recover Sputnik 5, carrying two dogs as passengers, Strelka and Belka

September 25: U.S. Atlas Able 5A, intended to be lunar probe, suffers launch failure

October 4: Courier 1B, an active repeater communications satellite, launched by U.S. Army

October 10-14: Attempts believed to be made by USSR to launch a Mars mission during visit of Khrushchev to the United Nations

October 13: NASA launches three mice, Amy, Sally, and Moe, in suborbital flight into space

December 1: Soviet Sputnik 6 is launched carrying two dogs, Pchelka and Mushka, but burns up on reentry

December 15: Atlas Able 5B also fails at launch. A two-year gap ensues before renewed lunar attempts with the U.S. Ranger and Soviet Luna lander series

December 19: NASA launches the first Mercury-Redstone capsule-launch vehicle combination for unmanned suborbital test flight

PART 2

SENDING HUMANS INTO SPACE

6

WINGS TOWARD SPACE: THE STORY OF THE X-15

I kind of felt like I was the first astronaut.
—Scott Crossfield
X-15 test pilot

The X-1: Breaking the "Barriers"

Could human beings fly into space in a winged vehicle, in some kind of rocket-powered airplane that could leave Earth's atmosphere, enter space and then return under its own control to land on a conventional or near-conventional runway?

Today, thanks to the successes of the U.S. Space Shuttle, we know that such flights can be made. Plans are on the drawing boards not only in the U.S., but also at other space centers around the world, for an even more advanced and sophisticated "space plane." This plane of the future will not only land on a runway, as the Shuttle does, but take off from one as well, then enter space under its own power and reenter the atmosphere for a powered return to Earth.

In the late 1950s, however, such dreams and successes were a long way away, and just getting a human being into space by any means possible was our greatest challenge.

While NASA was readying a small group of men called "The Mercury Seven" to meet this challenge by being lifted aloft in tiny "cabins" perched on top of giant rockets, another group, working at Edwards Air Force Base deep in the Mojave Desert in California,

dreamed of "flying" into space in an experimental aircraft called the X-15.

A tiny, sleek, rocket-powered airplane shaped like a 50-caliber bullet, the X-15 was the last in a line of rocket-powered aircraft developed by the United States to test and expand the limits of aircraft. As humankind reached outward and upward to greater speeds and altitudes in its attempt to free itself from the Earth, a small group of experimenters and pilots were betting on "winging" it—making it to space with a winged aircraft.

In fact, from the mid-1940s when the series started until the late 1960s when it ended, these sleek, fast, experimental aircraft broke human records and nature's boundaries during America's golden age of experimental aircraft flight. It was an astounding time for aviation, and until the program was eclipsed by the thunder of bigger rockets from Cape Canaveral, these pilots flew faster and higher than ever before . . . and they almost reached the heavens.

The program had started during the '40s with the development of the X-1. Designed to examine the problems of supersonic flight, the X-1 had one major objective: to break "the sound barrier"—Mach 1, or the speed of sound—a speed at which aircraft became unstable, shook violently and, many people believed, would quite literally fall apart. By the mid-1940s the "sound barrier" had assumed almost mythic proportions. Better aircraft materials, higher-efficiency fuel, more sophisticated technology and ever increasing know-how were dictating that aircraft could and should fly faster and higher, but the "barrier," the "wall," was always there in front to stop them. Some pilots and engineers believed that it would never be scaled.

On October 14, 1947, test pilot Charles (Chuck) Yeager proved them wrong. Strapped securely into the cockpit of the X-1 and nursing a couple of ribs badly injured in a fall from horseback a few days before, Yeager and his craft were carried aloft and launched from the belly of a B-29. The four-barreled liquid-oxygen and ethyl-alcohol engine kicked in and Yeager pushed his aircraft, nicknamed "Glamorous Glennis" after his wife, to a speed of 700 miles an hour—just past Mach 1. The sound barrier was broken in both actual and psychological fact. After the violent buffeting "the airplane smoothed out just as slick as glass," Yeager reported later. There was no invisible wall, no law of nature to stop pilot and plane anymore. Within months the goal was no longer to make the once "impossible" Mach 1, but to fly even faster and higher. Once freed, the bird now had to test its wings. In dozens of tests the X-1 and later experimental aircraft now pushed toward the limit of their endurance. In November 1953 Yeager's comrade and rival, test pilot Scott Crossfield, climbed into a Douglas Skyrocket and after trying and failing six times to push past Mach 2, finally put the plane into a 72,000-foot dive and broke the record—traveling

faster than 1,291 miles an hour, more than twice the speed of sound.

The X-2: Beyond Mach 2

If two, why not three? The next rocket-plane in the series, the X-2, was designed to do just that, to fly at three times the speed of sound and climb to an altitude of 130,000 feet. Carried aloft by a B-50 bomber, the X-2 had stainless-steel wings and an aluminum-steel alloy fuselage. Some pilots also thought it had a jinx. High over Lake Ontario, on May 13, 1953, as it was about to begin its first powered flight test it exploded, killing test pilot Skip Ziegler and one member of the B-50 crew.

The tests were moved back to Edwards in 1954, and Air Force Lieutenant Colonel Pat Everest, Jr., took over the controls for the X-2's second test flight. On July 23, 1956, Everest set a speed record of Mach 2.93 and climbed to an altitude of 75,000 feet. On September 7, 1956, Captain Ivan C. Kincheloe flew to a record height of 126,200 feet, and 20 days later, on September 27, 1956, Captain Milburn Apt pushed the X-2 to an incredible speed of 3.196 Mach or 2,094 miles an hour. A few seconds later the plane went out of control, killing Apt as it crashed into the desert floor.

Nonetheless, Mach 3 had been achieved, and in some ways an era had ended. The X-2 had done its job, although not without tragedy. With the next aircraft in the series, the most advanced airplane of all time, the X-15, a new objective would be defined, heroically achieved and then frustratingly abandoned.

Mach 1 and the "Sonic Barrier"

Named in honor of the Austrian physicist Ernst Mach (1838-1916), "Mach" numbers simply express the speed of an aircraft or other object in ratio to the speed of sound in the same medium, such as air or water. At sea level under normal conditions sound travels through the air at about 1,086 feet (331 meters) per second. An aircraft traveling at this same speed is said to be flying at *Mach 1*. Flying less than Mach 1, an aircraft is said to be *subsonic*; flying at greater than Mach 1, *supersonic*.

Since sound travels in waves through a medium, the

speed of sound may vary according to the nature, temperature and density of the medium.

The so-called *sonic barrier* at Mach 1 is the result of the sudden increase in air resistance met by an aircraft as it approaches the speed of sound. At such speeds shock waves form and turbulence battering the aircraft becomes severe. A *sonic boom* is generated when such a supersonic aircraft overtakes the pressure waves it produces, creating a loud noise in the form of a shock wave cone.

Courtesy, Edwards AFB

Charles "Chuck" Yeager with the X-1, "Glamorous Glennis," named for his wife

The X-15: Traveling to the Edge of Space

The official agenda of the X-15 was clear-cut and demanding. The small, black, bullet-shaped, rocket-powered craft was to use its 1-million horsepower engine to travel twice as fast as a rifle bullet and investigate problems of manned flight in a near-space environment. Its objectives were to fly up to an altitude of 50 miles (264,000 feet), and to reach speeds of Mach 6.

With a little luck and a lot of skill the X-15 could be the first rocket-powered spacecraft, designed to fly into space (but not orbit) and then return in controlled flight. Quite simply, many of the pilots, engineers and scientists on the project believed that the X-15 would first take humankind into space.

Looking like a baby's toy compared to today's Space Shuttle, the X-15, carrying its liquid-oxygen and alcohol fuel, was to be tucked under the wing of a B-52 for its journey aloft. Upon release it would fire its engine, make its flight, and then return to the dry lake runway in the Mojave Desert at Edwards. Painted black to radiate heat back into the atmosphere during its reentry, the craft was also cooled by a liquid-nitrogen cooling system.

Scott Crossfield, who had left the government and gone to work for the X-15's contractor, North American Aviation, was the first to fly the new rocket-plane on June 8, 1959. "I kind of felt I was the first astronaut," Scott Crossfield recalled in a television interview years later. After a long series of test flights in which the X-15 never left its cradled position under the wing of the B-52, the first "free" flights were

merely glide tests as Crossfield brought the craft back home to the landing strip at Edwards. The first actual powered flight, using two X-1 engines instead of the big, 1-million horsepower engine that was still not ready, took place on September 17, 1959. "It wasn't easy to fly, but it was an honest airplane," Crossfield later said.

Nonetheless the X-15 was an experimental airplane. On November 5, 1959, an engine failure caused a small fire in the aircraft. Crossfield at the controls took the plane into a dive but he couldn't jettison the heavy and highly explosive fuel. Luckily, the fire died out, but on landing the X-15 broke cleanly in two, just inches behind the cockpit and ahead of the fuel tank. Crossfield walked away unharmed and three weeks later the "design oversight" in the broken-backed plane had been corrected and it was back on line for another flight.

By late November of 1960 the big engine had arrived and the X-15 was complete. "All the pieces were in place. It was the world series," Crossfield recalled. With its 1-million horsepower engine installed, the tiny X-15 had three times the power of the Navy's Vanguard rocket and burned a ton of fuel in 11 seconds. Capable of flying at six times the speed of sound, it might have been America's first space plane, but such fame wasn't in store.

With one more flight on his schedule before North American turned the X-15 over to NASA for government testing, Crossfield had one last chance to push the plane to its limits, to fly faster and higher than any human had ever done before—to aim for the heavens and become the first human, American or Russian, in space.

Pilot Scott Crossfield with the X-15

In December 1960 Crossfield was to make his last flight in the craft he had developed from its infancy. Over the past 18 months he had flown the X-15 in 13 of its 29 test flights, but his orders now were to go "low and slow." Would Crossfield follow orders now and reign in the X-15, or would he open up the rocketplane to its full potential and break for the heavens? On the ground they were betting money, but in the cockpit there wasn't any decision to be made. Scott Crossfield was a professional test pilot and test pilots followed orders and did their job the way it was supposed to be done. The X-15 was turned over to NASA's test pilots for further tests and Scott Crossfield would not become America's first man in space.

Days of Thunder and Glory

Between 1960, when it was turned over to the government, and 1967, when it made its last flight, the X-15 continued to assault and break records for speed and altitude. Already, on May 12, 1960, Joe Walker had flown the X-15 to Mach 3.19, equalling Mel Apt's record set in the X-1 three years before, and in August Walker hit Mach 3.31. In February 1961, Robert White broke through to Mach 3.5 and less than three weeks later, on March 7, 1961, hit Mach 4.43. In a burst of record-shattering unprecedented in aviation history, White then hit Mach 4.62 six weeks later. Mach 5 was exceeded by White on June 23 with a speed of 3,603 miles (5,798 km) an hour (Mach 5.27) and that record, too, was broken in flights by Forrest Peterson and Joe Walker in September and October that reached Mach 5.3 and 5.73. On November 9, 1961, White pushed the X-15 to its limit, reaching Mach 6.04, or 4,093 miles

(6,587 km) an hour. Finally, on October 3, 1967, William Knight hit the fastest speed in the X-15 series, Mach 6.7, or 4,520 miles (7,274 km) an hour.

Faster than any aircraft had ever flown before, the X-15 also aimed for the heavens. On August 12, 1960, as it flew at ever higher altitudes, Robert White reached 136,499 feet (41,605 m) and on March 30, 1961, Walker climbed to 169,600 feet (51,594 m), more than 32 miles. White then reached 217,000 feet (66,142 m) and in April of 1962 Walker pushed to 246,700 feet (75,194 m). Then 314,750 feet (95,936 m) followed—more than 59 miles high—in the first unofficial "spaceflight" flown by White, and an all-time world altitude record was set in August of 1963 when the X-15 was pushed by Walker to an incredible height of 354,300 feet (107,991 m) or 67 miles.

By the end of the program on October 3, 1967, the X-15 had been put through 199 flights, breaking all existing records for speed and altitude and supplying new and valuable information on the effects (both on human and machine) of high-speed flight in a near-space environment. One man had been lost, test pilot Michael Adams, in flight number 191 in November 1967.

The X-15 had met and surpassed all of its goals. It was the most successful high-performance experimental aircraft in aviation history. Did it reach space? The United States Air Force said yes, NASA said no. In the early 1960s the Air Force had decided that flights over 50 miles in altitude qualified as space flights and created a special astronaut rating for pilots who flew them. Under the Air Force standard, 13 different flights flown by test pilots Joe Walker, Robert White, Robert Rushford, Joe Engle, John McKay, William Dana, William Knight and Michael Adams

NASA

X-15 being released from the wing of its B-52 "mother ship."

qualified. White, Rushford, Engle, Knight and Adams were awarded Air Force Astronaut wings. As civilians, Walker, McKay and Dana were not eligible.

However, the international standard set by the Fédération Astronautique Internationale (FAI), which NASA adheres to, recognizes only those flights over 62 miles (100 km) as spaceflights. By those rules only Joe Walker of the X-15 pilots qualifies, which he did in two of his flights.

Could the X-15 have reached any higher? The question would never be answered. NASA had already focused on Project Mercury instead, and had put the first American in space not aboard a plane, but in a ballistic re-entry spacecraft that plummeted to Earth like a bullet instead of flying back from space. This decision effectively had curtailed exploration of other possibilities. The pursuit of the X-15 technology was abandoned, and although the experimental rocket-plane yielded much information that would be useful later in the development of the Space Shuttle, it would never become a true spacecraft.

7

THE FIRST HUMANS IN SPACE: VOSTOK AND MERCURY

To be the first to enter the cosmos, to engage, single-handed, in an unprecedented duel with nature—could one dream of anything more?
—Yuri Gagarin,
the first human in space, prior to lift-off

Even as the X-rocket-plane test pilots soared to break record after record, their conquests still remained for the most part in the realm of aviation—flight through the atmosphere. For both the U.S. and the USSR, the long-held dream of human spaceflight still lay ahead.

To achieve that goal both countries would settle, not on a plane like the X-15, but on a "ballistic spacecraft," lobbed beyond the atmosphere by a rocket much in the same way they had already sent tiny orbiting satellites into space.

While sending a shiny piece of aluminum up into orbit had been an exhilarating first, that undertaking didn't compare in complexity with sending a human being into space. When Vanguard blew up, it cost money, caused embarrassment, and set back the U.S. space program, but the loss did not include a human life. What's more, before we started sending people into space, no one, Soviet or American, knew exactly what would happen to the human body in the weightlessness of space (although the X-15 pilots had explored some of the implications).

In addition, humans in space would need food, water, oxygen, air pressure, heat and a method for disposing of waste. Too much acceleration on the ascent could destroy living tissues. Excessive heat on reentry into the atmosphere could be equally devas-

tating. There had to be escape systems and a way to recover the spacecraft and rescue its human cargo, as well as a rocket powerful enough to hurl a human being into orbit.

Both countries were undaunted by these challenges. In the U.S., in one of its first actions as far back as October 7, 1958, NASA had formally approved Project Mercury, which would set out to orbit a man in space around the Earth. In the USSR, testing began as early as May 1960 for the first manned flight, in a spacecraft called Vostok.

Precursors to Human Flight

During the same years that both Soviets and Americans were achieving firsts with satellites and lunar probes, both countries actively explored the possibilities of human space flight.

By April 2, 1959, NASA had chosen its first seven astronauts—the Mercury Seven. They were all seasoned military test pilots, including representatives from the U.S. Air Force (L. Gordon Cooper, Virgil I. "Gus" Grissom and Donald K. "Deke" Slayton), from the U.S. Navy (M. Scott Carpenter, Alan B. Shepard, Jr. and Walter M. Schirra, Jr.) and from the U.S. Marine Corps (John H. Glenn, Jr.).

The harsh and unforgiving environment of space would have to be tested first. In fact, even before Laika's trip aboard Sputnik 2, both Soviets and Americans had tried sending various animals up to very high suborbital altitudes (that is, into the edges of space, but not far enough to be pulled into orbit around the Earth. Instead, these early shots plummeted right back down to the ground or ocean). In the USSR, tests with animals began as early as 1949. By 1951, the U.S. had placed a compartment holding several mice and a monkey on top of a small rocket and sent it spaceward. They were the first living creatures to make it back to Earth alive.

Other animals were lost. In the U.S., in December 1958, a nosecone containing a squirrel monkey named "Old Reliable" was lost at sea after launch by a Jupiter IRBM (intermediate range ballistic missile) at Cape Canaveral. In May 1959 two monkeys, Able and Baker, made it home safely, but Able died on the operating table when bioelectrodes (the sensors that had recorded his biological reactions) were being removed from his body. In December 1959 and January 1960, however, two rhesus monkeys, Sam and Miss Sam, were each recovered in tests to see if the Mercury capsule and its passengers could survive a mission that had been aborted, or cancelled, after launch. An October 1960 test sent three mice, Amy, Sally, and Moe, on a successful suborbital flight including 20 minutes of weightlessness when their great altitude took them beyond gravity's relentless pull.

By now the U.S. Mercury program was closing in on manned flight. An unmanned Mercury capsule followed in a suborbital flight in December, and January 31, 1961, saw another Mercury capsule carry Ham, a 137-pound (62 kg) chimpanzee, into a suborbital flight path 155 miles (249 km) in altitude. Launched by a Redstone rocket (MR-2) at Cape Canaveral, Ham came through with flying colors.

Meanwhile, between November 3, 1957, and March 25, 1961, the Soviets sent seven dogs into space to probe the biological hazards. Laika in Sputnik 2, had proved that a living organism could survive the trip up into space and could journey there for up to 10 days. Three years later, in 1960, two more dogs traveled in Sputnik 5—Belka (Squirrel) and Strelka (Little Arrow)—descending safely after 18 orbits and proving for the first time that it was also possible to make it home from an orbital flight in one piece. Their craft was a prototype of the Vostok spacecraft that would later carry the USSR's first cosmonauts into space.

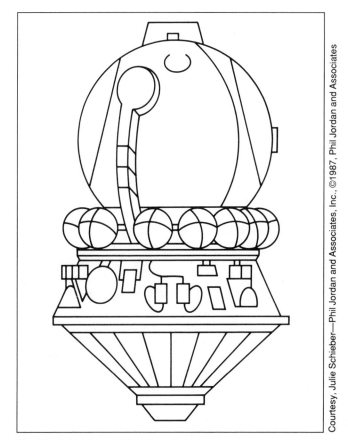

The Vostok spacecraft

Two other canine cosmonauts died like Laika, however, for the cause—Pohelka (Little Bee) and Mushka (Little Fly)—perishing when their craft, Sputnik 6, burned up in the atmosphere because of an error in the descent angle. Two others came down safely in March 1961 after one orbit—Chernushka (Blackie), a passenger in Sputnik 9, and Zvezdochka (Little Star), who rode with a dummy cosmonaut aboard Sputnik 10.

Between August 21, 1959, and April 28, 1961, the U.S. ran 17 tests of various kinds for the Mercury program. They checked escape systems, controls, heat protection on reentry, aerodynamics and recovery, as well as the effects of ascent, suborbital flight and descent on test monkeys, simulated human pilots and Ham the chimp. The Mercury program had faced many frustrations though—only 10 of these tests were successful—and Ham's flight in January 1961 was still only suborbital, even though the first U.S. orbital flight had originally been planned for April 1960.

Still, in both Soviet and American programs human space flight seemed just around the corner.

Yuri's Triumph

On April 12, 1961, Radio Moscow announced to all the world: Yuri A. Gagarin was the first human ever to travel in space.

The historic flight began with lift-off at Tyuratam at 10:55 A.M., Moscow time. As the engines rumbled more than 98 feet (30 m) below him and the Vostok spacecraft lifted skyward atop the modified A-1 ICBM, Gagarin yelled an excited, "Poyekhali!" (Let's go!). He then felt the tremendous crush of the lift-off force pushing him downward into the metallic structure of his ejector seat. Just a half-minute later, traveling now faster than sound, all sound stopped for him, and the spacecraft seemed to be moving back and forth as if on the end of a spring. Gagarin could feel the acceleration decrease sharply as the booster rockets shut down and he heard the far-away sound of latches unfastening as the spent rockets dropped away. Twice more, as the core booster and the second stage each burned, he would be alternately pressed back hard against the ejector seat, and then pitched forward. A roaring sound, disconcertingly close, signaled the jettisoning of the protective shroud around his spacecraft.

Then, without warning, he felt the engine shut down and all objects seemed suspended in midair. Gagarin and his Vostok spacecraft had entered orbit around the Earth; his arms, notebooks, pens floated loose in the strange world of weightlessness and the vast expanse of space. He would complete a single orbit around the Earth in a voyage that lasted just one hour and 48 minutes. It was a voyage that the world would never forget.

The Nedelin Disaster

Gagarin's flight was a triumph made even more courageous coming as it did on the heels of a Soviet tragedy that few people outside the USSR knew anything about at the time.

During his visit to the United Nations the previous fall, Soviet Premier Nikita Khrushchev had indicated that he expected yet another Soviet success in space to occur while he was in New York. Nothing happened, however, and puzzled Western observers watched the Soviet space tracking ships turn around and head for home, mission apparently unaccomplished. Meanwhile, an irritable Khrushchev packed up his things and returned to Moscow in mid-October.

Years later it came out that, apparently, after two failed attempts to launch a probe to the planet Mars during what's called the "window of opportunity" (when a launch from Earth can reach it using the least power and fuel) in fall 1960, which coincided with Khrushchev's trip, the pressure on Soviet space experts was immense. Field Marshal Mitrofan Nedelin, distraught that a third rocket launch attempt refused to fire, ordered technicians out onto the launch pad to examine the dud. To encourage them, he accompanied the foray. Moments later the rocket suddenly ignited in a huge blast that killed many of the top Soviet space engineers in a single horrible blast. Nothing was mentioned in the Soviet press at the time, but over the years news about this "Nedelin Disaster" has slowly leaked out. Even today that tragedy may stand as the worst in the history of space exploration.

The First Space Pilots

The U.S., meanwhile, was proceeding with judicious caution. The Redstone rocket, designed by von Braun and his team for lobbing the satellite Explorer into orbit, was powerful enough to send a manned Mercury capsule into suborbital flight, but not into orbit. For that job, like the Soviets, NASA planned to make use of a modified ICBM, the Atlas rocket. While tests of the Mercury capsule, the escape tower and the Mercury/Redstone combination went along reasonably well, the Mercury/Atlas interface was dogged with problems. The first test, on July 29, 1960, failed about 60 seconds after lift-off and only fragments were recovered at sea. The entire Mercury program hung in jeopardy when the second Mercury/Atlas test was readied in February 1961. This second test was a success but a third, launched with a dummy spaceman aboard 13 days after Gagarin's flight, slipped out of control and had to be destroyed.

At the same time, Ham's ride aboard the Mercury/Redstone combination in January had brought much more encouraging results. Both the capsule and its furry "astronaut" had done fine, but von Braun was concerned about over-acceleration and vibration problems in the Redstone and added an extra test in March before he would okay the project for manned flight. This extra test went well, and some commentators speculate that, had NASA taken the risk, the U.S. could have put a man in space in March—before Gagarin's flight.

The first American astronaut in space was Alan B. Shepard. Because of his reputation as a crack test pilot and engineer, he had been chosen for the first Mercury flight by vote of his fellow astronauts and NASA officials. Shepard crawled into the tiny 9 1/2- foot tall capsule, which he had dubbed "Freedom 7," on the

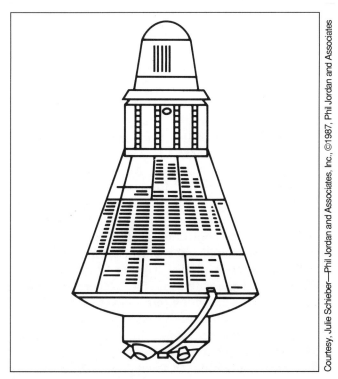

Mercury spacecraft

morning of May 5, 1961. Four hours and many delays later, observers at the Cape Canaveral, Florida, launch site saw clouds of oxygen vapor engulf the towering white Redstone rocket, its cargo perched on its nose as the countdown reached lift-off and Shepard's comparatively calm report from inside, "Ahh, Roger; lift-off and the clock has started . . . Yes, sir, reading you loud and clear. This is Freedom 7."

Inside, Shepard was pressed back onto his seat by the tremendous force of the rocket as it sped to 5,180 mph and lifted to 116.5 miles above the Earth's surface before the engines cut off and the booster rocket dropped away to leave astronaut and capsule on their own. Hurtling through space at more than four times the speed of sound, Shepard tested the manual altitude controls, later reporting that ". . . movement was smooth and could be controlled precisely."

Mercury then automatically positioned itself for descent, bottom downward, its heat shield—which would be more crucial on return from later, orbital flights—in place. Its three retro-rockets fired (a reverse blast to brake the speed), followed by a parachute, which opened at 21,000 feet to steady the craft, and the main parachute at 10,000 feet to slow its descent. Freedom 7 dropped neatly down into the Atlantic Ocean just 40 miles from target. Within 25 minutes after lift-off, Alan Shepard was on board the

recovery ship, ready for a congratulatory phone call from President John F. Kennedy. The entire flight had lasted 15 minutes, 22 seconds.

Buoyed by Shepard's success, three weeks later Kennedy would make his historic announcement of U.S. intentions to put a man on the moon. The Mercury program now became, not just a self-contained effort to put humans in space, but the threshold to the future. The U.S. manned space program had been born.

On July 21, 1961, Virgil I. ("Gus") Grissom piloted "Liberty Bell 7" in the second U.S. suborbital flight. Once again, the flight went smoothly, with Grissom enjoying the sights through his window, but 15 minutes, 37 seconds after lift-off, as Grissom and capsule were floating in the Atlantic Ocean, ready to be picked up, the hatch release blew prematurely and Liberty Bell 7 began taking on huge quantities of water. Thinking fast, Grissom dived out through the hatch and bobbed in the cold water as a Marine Corps helicopter attempted to haul the capsule out of the ocean. The helicopter warning lights were flashing, though, and its pilot released the line. Liberty 7 sank into oblivion—the only manned spacecraft the U.S. lost in the Mercury, Gemini and Apollo programs. Moments later, and none too soon, a second helicopter fished the water-logged Grissom from the ocean as Americans breathed a sigh of relief.

The Soviets were first in space and American politicians were eager to see the U.S. catch up. While the Mercury program had not yet orbited an astronaut, Shepard and Grissom had become the first men actually to pilot a spacecraft, controlling its pitch, yaw and roll. Their flights were a good beginning.

Vostok 2

The political competition between the two countries in the realm of space triumphs had by now become intense. Soviet Premier Nikita Khrushchev had proudly presented U.S. President Dwight Eisenhower with a model of a lunar probe that had reached the moon during a summit meeting of the two leaders in Washington, D.C., in 1959, but the next year, strong evidence indicates, the Soviet program suffered setbacks from the Nedelin Disaster.

Despite that loss by spring 1961, with Gagarin's flight, the Soviets had clearly recouped lost ground. Following the U.S. suborbital flights in May and July, they continued their clear lead with a second manned spaceflight, this time for a full day in orbit, the flight lasting 25 hours, 18 minutes. Flown by Gherman Titov, Vostok 2 was launched August 6, 1961, completed 17 orbits around the Earth and was recovered successfully on August 7.

Glenn's Glory

Meanwhile, the problem of the Mercury/Atlas interface still haunted the U.S. program. Out of the three Mercury/Atlas tests conducted so far, only one had been successful. Unless NASA could get the Atlas rocket to work with the Mercury capsule, the whole orbital program was doomed. At last, on September 13, 1961, MA-4 made a successful single orbital flight with a simulated human pilot on board. On November 29, NASA sent a chimpanzee astronaut named Enos aboard MA-5 on what was to be a three-orbit test flight. Control problems forced Enos down after just two passes around the Earth, but NASA felt ready at last to send a human astronaut into orbit. John Glenn, the most experienced pilot of the "Seven," would have the honor.

Still, a lot of questions remained about exactly what effects the flight would have on Glenn. True, the Soviets had already put two humans in orbit, but Soviet secrecy about their internal affairs kept NASA completely in the dark about the effects on the cos-monauts themselves. What would prolonged exposure to weightlessness do? Would Glenn be able to function? What would happen to his eyesight, his heartbeat? What long-term effects might there be?

It took courage for John Glenn to crawl into that tiny capsule. In the early morning hours of February 20, 1962, after six delays because of bad weather and technical difficulties, the Americans got their turn to send a human orbiting in space around the Earth, and John Glenn got his chance. At 4:55 A.M. Glenn's "Friendship 7" lifted off to make three revolutions, orbiting like a tiny moon around the Earth.

The flight did not go off without a hitch, however. Early on, ground controllers noticed warning signals that indicated the all-important heat shield was loose. Without the heat shield in place Glenn would be literally fried on reentry into the Earth's atmosphere. Instead of jettisoning the retro-rockets as usual after firing them, Glenn was advised to keep them in place to help keep the heat shield from falling off. As he plummeted Earthward, flaming pieces of the retropack (containing the spent rockets) flew past his window. As it later turned out, the warning signals had been a false alarm and the heat shield was firmly in place, but for Glenn, the anxious ground controllers

John Glenn twisting into the "Friendship 7" Mercury capsule

NASA

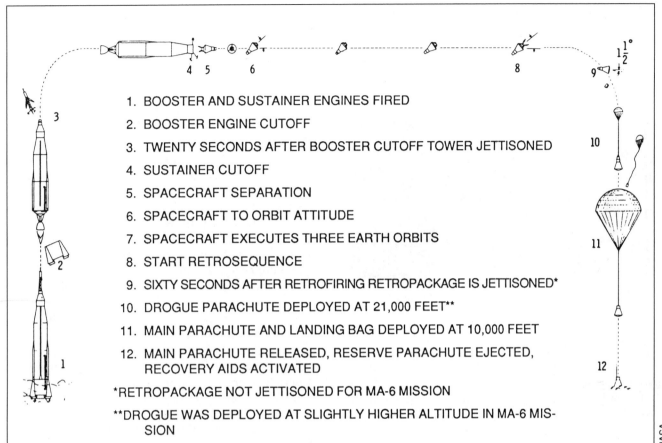

1. BOOSTER AND SUSTAINER ENGINES FIRED
2. BOOSTER ENGINE CUTOFF
3. TWENTY SECONDS AFTER BOOSTER CUTOFF TOWER JETTISONED
4. SUSTAINER CUTOFF
5. SPACECRAFT SEPARATION
6. SPACECRAFT TO ORBIT ATTITUDE
7. SPACECRAFT EXECUTES THREE EARTH ORBITS
8. START RETROSEQUENCE
9. SIXTY SECONDS AFTER RETROFIRING RETROPACKAGE IS JETTISONED*
10. DROGUE PARACHUTE DEPLOYED AT 21,000 FEET**
11. MAIN PARACHUTE AND LANDING BAG DEPLOYED AT 10,000 FEET
12. MAIN PARACHUTE RELEASED, RESERVE PARACHUTE EJECTED, RECOVERY AIDS ACTIVATED

*RETROPACKAGE NOT JETTISONED FOR MA-6 MISSION

**DROGUE WAS DEPLOYED AT SLIGHTLY HIGHER ALTITUDE IN MA-6 MIS-SION

NASA

Sequence of major events in a Mercury mission

and the waiting American public, the return flight was nerve-wracking. All went well, however, and Friendship 7 splashed down into the Atlantic four hours, 55 minutes, 23 seconds after lift-off.

John Glenn's return to Earth was greeted by Americans with wild enthusiasm. He was a national hero whose feat was seen on a par with Lindbergh's first flight across the Atlantic. Like Lindbergh and other national heroes, he was given a ticker-tape parade down the streets of New York to the welcome of thousands of cheering fans.

Later that spring, on the morning of May 24, astronaut Scott Carpenter flew the Mercury capsule Aurora 7 on a second three- orbit flight lasting four hours, 56 minutes, 5 seconds. Carpenter may have spent more time looking at the view than paying attention to his instrument panel, resulting in an oversight on his part, but in any case he had to fire the retro-rockets manually, and an attitude error caused the spacecraft to land 250 miles downrange from the spot where the recovery ships were waiting. It took almost three hours to complete the recovery, causing

TV commentator Walter Cronkite to worry on the air that "America may have lost an astronaut." Carpenter, however, crawled out onto a life raft and calmly waited for rescue ships to arrive.

Vostok 3/4

Meanwhile, the Soviet cosmonauts, who were already ahead of their U.S. counterparts in length of missions, number of orbits and hours logged in space, continued to impress the world with space feats. On August 11 and August 12, 1962, two Vostoks went on dual missions, both orbiting at once, communicating with each other by radio and telecasting to Earth. Soviet cosmonaut Andrian Nicolayev spent four days in space aboard Vostok 3, while Papel Popovich spent three days on Vostok 4. The spacecrafts landed within six minutes of each other, though 190 miles apart.

The Soviets would follow with another double flight in 1963. Cosmonaut Valery Bykovsky orbited Earth 81 times in a five-day flight aboard Vostok 5, beginning June 14, but it was the companion flight of Vostok 6

Yuri Gagarin and Valentina Tereshkova, first man and woman in space, wave to admiring fans

Tass from Sovfoto

that caught the attention of the world—with cosmonaut Valentina Tereshkova aboard, the first woman in space.

Tereshkova, who lifted off on June 16, made 48 revolutions around the Earth, and landed 70 hours, 50 minutes later on June 19, gave women the world over the sense that space belonged to both men and women. As former U.S. congresswoman and former ambassador Clare Boothe Luce told *Life* magazine, "The flight of Valentina Tereshkova is, consequently, symbolic of the emancipation of the Communist woman. It symbolizes to Russian women that they actively share in the glory of conquering space." The triumph was short-lived, however. It would be another 19 years before the Soviets would send another woman into space, and 20 before the U.S. would do so. Today, numerous women have an active part in the U.S. astronaut corps and Canada, Japan, France and Indonesia all have women training for future space missions. The future should see many more following suit.

Mercury Program Draws to a Close

The U.S. Mercury program wrapped up in the fall of 1962 and spring of 1963 with two more orbital flights.

Walter M. Schirra, Jr., took "Sigma 7" on a six-orbit flight on October 3. It lasted nine hours, 13 minutes, 11 seconds. The only major problem he encountered was difficulty regulating the temperature of his silvery space suit (which heated to an uncomfortable

89.6°F (32°C) before he was able to cool it down), and he splashed down neatly in the Pacific Ocean only 4 1/2 miles from the recovery ship.

In the final Mercury flight, astronaut L. Gordon Cooper flew "Faith 7" on the longest U.S. space voyage up to that point—whizzing around the Earth 22 times in a mission lasting more than a day, a total of 34 hours, 19 minutes, 49 seconds. Lifting off on May 15, 1963, Cooper's job was to report back to Earth on his physical condition and to manage his own supplies—such as electricity, oxygen and water. He was the first American astronaut to go to sleep in orbit. Cooper also reported details he saw on the Earth's surface—including the wake of a boat on a river in India and houses on the plains of Tibet—most of which experts didn't believe until reports like these were later corroborated by other astronauts.

During the flight a short circuit problem developed in the spacecraft and Cooper, like Carpenter, had to use manual retrofire and reentry but, like Schirra, he succeeded in coming within 4 1/2 miles of his splashdown target in the Pacific. In this single flight, Cooper had spent more time in space than all five previous American astronauts combined.

Cooper's flight signaled the end of the Mercury program, an effort that had lasted for over four years and had seen 25 flights, six of them manned. American astronauts had logged nearly 54 hours in space and had orbited Earth a total of 34 times. Of the original "Mercury Seven," only Deke Slayton had not had his day in space (because of medical problems). He would wait another 12 years before he would finally get his chance aboard the Apollo-Soyuz Test Project in 1975. Grissom would later die in the ill-fated Apollo fire at Cape Kennedy. Cooper would come back to command a later Gemini flight. Wally Schirra would return to space at the helm of both a Gemini and Apollo flight, and Shepard would return to command the Apollo 14 mission to the Moon.

In the same span of time, the Soviet cosmonauts had logged 259 orbits and 382 hours in space, including two dual flights. They had found out that humans could survive in space for as long as five days and that women could travel in space as well as men.

Additionally, the American astronauts had found that a human could function in the weightlessness of space as a pilot, engineer and experimenter, and could make important decisions even under the stress of this alien environment. The duration of their flights was shorter, but Americans pointed with pride to the pilot expertise they saw in their astronauts. In both countries the heroes of a new age had been born: the first human travelers in space.

Milestones In Space: Vostok And Mercury, 1961-1963

1961   January 31: The chimpanzee Ham makes his debut aboard U.S. spacecraft Mercury 2 in a 16 1/2-minute flight, transmitting signals from space and being successfully recovered after splashdown

March 9: Sputnik 9 carries Chernushka (Blackie) the dog aloft for the Soviets

April 12: Soviet cosmonaut Yuri Gagarin becomes the first human in space as he makes a single orbit of Earth in a 108-minute flight aboard Vostok 1

May 5: Alan Shepard becomes the second human in space and the first American astronaut in a 15-minute suborbital flight as pilot of the Mercury spacecraft Freedom 7, launched by a Redstone booster

July 21: U.S. astronaut Gus Grissom makes a 16-minute suborbital flight on Mercury 4 mission dubbed Liberty Bell 7.

August 7: Cosmonaut Gherman Titov completes 17 orbits of Earth flying Vostok 2 in the first day-long manned space flight.

November 29: U.S. puts Enos the chimpanzee into orbit on Mercury 5 mission for a two-revolution orbit

1962   February 20: In a 4 1/2-hour, three-orbit mission, John Glenn pilots Mercury spacecraft Friendship 7 to become the first American to orbit the Earth

May 24: Scott Carpenter takes the Aurora 7 Mercury spacecraft for a three-orbit flight

August 11: Soviet cosmonaut Andrian Nicolayev spends four days in space aboard Vostok 3, making radio contact with Vostok 4 and telecast to Earth

August 12: Soviet cosmonaut Papel Popovich pilots Vostok 4 in first double flight—in orbit at the same time as Nicolayev's Vostok 3

October 3: Mercury spacecraft Sigma 7, piloted by U.S. astronaut Wally Schirra, makes 6 orbits

1963   May 15: U.S. astronaut Gordon Cooper takes Mercury spacecraft Faith 7 up for 22 1/2 orbits

June 14: Soviet cosmonaut Valery Bykovsky orbits Earth 81 times, traveling a total of 2,046,000 miles (3,292,628 km) aboard Vostok 5 and returning June 19

June 16: The Soviets' Vostok 6 carries into orbit the world's first woman spacefarer, Valentina Tereshkova, for 48 revolutions around Earth in 70 hours, 50 minutes, also landing June 19

The Vostok Spacecraft

Country: USSR

Crew: One

Modules: Two, a reentry capsule and an equipment module

Reentry Capsule: Diameter: 7.5 ft. (2.3 m). Weight: 5,291 lb. (2,400 kg)
Equipment Module: Diameter: 7.9 ft. (2.4 m). Height: 8.5 ft. (2.58 m)

Total Height: 14.1 ft. (4.3 m)

Total Weight: 10,417 lb. (4,725 kg)[*]

[*] *Using Yuri Gagarin's Vostok 1 spacecraft as an example*

Designed by Soviet master spacecraft designer Sergei Korolev, the Vostok spacecraft was made up of two modules, a spherical reentry capsule, which carried its human passengers, and a cone-shaped equipment module. The versatile design would provide the basis for assembly-line production of a long generation of satellites in the Soviet space program.

Like the U.S. Mercury capsule, the Vostok spacecraft was launched atop a modified intercontinental ballistic missile, the five-stage A-1. Outside the two modules, a shroud protected the spacecraft during ascent through the atmosphere and was blasted free by solid propellant rockets once the spacecraft was above the denser layers of atmosphere.

Inside the round, pressurized cabin, the cosmonaut rode seated in an ejection seat opposite a circular hatch, with a view through three portholes. The ejection seat offered a means of escape, through a cutout in the shroud, in the event of a lift-off emergency and also provided transportation back to Earth at the end of the mission.

After lift-off, once beyond the atmosphere the two modules orbited together. But, unlike the U.S. Mercury capsule, Vostok was designed to fly on automatic, directed entirely by ground control, although in an emergency the cosmonaut could use a hand control to align the spacecraft's attitude manually. This difference may reflect the Soviet preference for group organization over reliance on individuals, or it may indicate Korolev's trust in the technology developed by his program. In either case, the philosophy of ground control automation continues to permeate most of the Soviet space program.

In preparation for reentry, the automatic orientation system switched on, retro-rockets fired and the spacecraft decelerated. As the descent began, the instrument section was jettisoned, leaving the spherical reentry module to plummet downward alone. It orientated itself aerodynamically (it had no attitude control systems other than its offset center of mass), its ablative coating protecting it against the searing heat.

Following the course of Gagarin's Vostok 1 spacecraft as a typical example, at 22,966 ft. (7,000 m)

the hatch on the reentry sphere was jettisoned, and the cosmonaut in his seat was ejected two seconds later. Braked by a small parachute, the cosmonaut descended to an altitude of 13,123 ft. (4,000 m), where his ejection seat was jettisoned and a parachute deployed as he approached the ground. Meanwhile, the spacecraft, descending separately, jettisoned a second hatch, also at 13,123 ft. (4,000 m), and deployed a braking chute. At 8,202 ft. (2,500 m) the main spacecraft parachute deployed as the module streaked earthward. Because the reentry module's landing impact was too great to be safe for humans, all the Vostok cosmonauts ejected from the reentry module in this way and parachuted down separately.

Although the longest Vostok mission lasted five days, as a safety precaution, the Vostok life-support systems were designed to last 10 days and the spacecraft carried 10 days' worth of supplies. The Vostoks were all injected into orbits that would decay naturally within that 10-day period. Additionally, the ejection seat was equipped with emergency food rations and a dingy—just in case a cosmonaut landed on water instead of the vast expanses of the Soviet plains, as planned.

In all, the Vostok program included six spaceflights carrying human cosmonauts, including the first man in space, the first to spend a full day in space, two paired missions (3/4 and 5/6), and the first woman in space. From its first human flight to the final one, the program lasted 26 months.

The Mercury Spacecraft

Country: U.S.

Crew: One

Modules: One

Weight: 4,256 lb. (1,934 kg), at lift-off, including escape tower;* 2,987 lb. (1,355 kg), in orbit; 2,493 lb. (1,130 kg), at splashdown
Height: 26 ft. (7.9 m), including escape tower and aerodynamic spike at tip; 9.51 ft. (2.9 m), just the capsule

Width: 74.5 in. (189 cm), across the heat shield

The first U.S. spacecraft, Mercury, was a capsule designed to carry one human pilot into space. The six astronauts who commanded Mercury missions traveled on their backs, wedged in at the wide end of the bell-shaped craft. Each one rode in a custom-molded seat to make sure that the heavy increase in Earth's gravitational pull on lift-off was evenly distributed on the astronaut's body. Because of the cramped quarters, all seven of the astronauts chosen for the Mercury program measured less than 5 feet 11 inches.

Traveling in Mercury's pressurized cabin, the astronauts did not have to pressurize their suits

*
Using John Glenn's Friendship 7 (MA-6) as an example

during the entire flight. If they needed to, however, just lowering the helmet visor caused the suits to pressurize.

Inside, directly above the astronaut, were the main instrument consoles. The astronauts could control the pitch, yaw and roll of the spacecraft with a three-axis manual control. A porthole provided one view out, while a periscope display provided another.

Each manned mission was named by its pilot, beginning with astronaut Alan Shepard's first flight, which he dubbed "Freedom 7," possibly because it was the seventh capsule atop the seventh Redstone booster, possibly because there were seven astronauts in the Mercury team, or just possibly because pilots sometimes tend to be superstitious. In any case, all the others followed suit with "7" in their call names: Gus Grissom's mission was "Liberty Bell 7"; John Glenn's, "Friendship 7"; Scott Carpenter's, "Aurora 7"; Wally Schirra's, "Sigma 7"; and Gordon Cooper's, "Faith 7."

For all manned Mercury flights, either a Redstone or Atlas rocket provided the boost into space. In case of problems with the booster rocket on lift-off, an escape rocket tower extending from the top of the Mercury capsule was poised to pull capsule and pilot out of danger. (This system never came into play, however, except in testing.) When not needed, the escape tower was jettisoned after blast-off.

The double-walled capsule was made of nickle-alloy, with an outer skin of titanium to protect against the extreme heat of reentry, reinforced by a special heat shield at the base of the bell.

For the return trip, the thrusters positioned Mercury at the proper angle, followed by firing of the three solid-propellant retro-rockets, which then separated. As Mercury plummeted base downward toward Earth it gathered a speed of some 15,000 mph. At an altitude of about 25 miles the heat shield became critical to survival as it became subjected to a temperature of up to 1,650 degrees C.

As the capsule continued downward through the atmosphere a drogue parachute played out behind to slow the speed. The heat shield then dropped down about 4 feet from the bottom of the bell to deploy a landing bag that cushioned the impact on splash-down. The parachute detached right after landing, and the capsule's natural buoyance kept it bobbing in the ocean (in all but one manned mission) until naval recovery ships arrived.

A total of 15 Mercury capsules, produced by Mc-Donnell-Douglas, were used in manned and unmanned flights (some made more than one flight for a total of 25 test flights in all).

8

MORE, FARTHER, LONGER: VOSKHOD AND GEMINI

> *W*e are gliding across the world in total silence, with absolute smoothness; a motion of stately grace which makes me feel godlike as I stand erect in my sideways chariot, cruising the night sky.
> —Michael Collins describing his Gemini 10 space walk in his book *Carrying the Fire*

By 1964, a year after the last Vostok and Mercury missions, the competition to win points with space successes had intensified both in the Soviet Union and the United States. More than 20 years after the fact, it now seems clear that Soviet Premier Nikita Khrushchev had commandeered most of the previous Soviet successes for political purposes. Faced with imminent defeat from within the Communist party, Khrushchev desperately needed another success. Ever since the last Vostok mission he'd been pushing his lead designer, the brilliant Sergei Korolev, to come up with a way to send three men into space—and soon—to one-up the Americans, who were working step-by-step toward a mission to the Moon.

Since the next-generation spacecraft (the Soyuz) would need several years of development yet, Korolev apparently adapted the trusty Vostok for the job. The ejection seat was removed and a third cosmonaut was squeezed in a little in front of the other two. The capsule was so cramped for three crewmen that no room was left for space suits—or for extra emergency supplies. Everything would have to go smoothly, or the cosmonauts would not survive, but the Soviets decided to take a risk.

Voskhod 1: Three Men in a Spaceship

On October 12, 1964, after two unmanned test missions by similar spacecraft, the first revamped Vostok, called Voskhod 1 (meaning "Sunrise"), blasted into orbit. Aboard, it carried the world's first three-man crew, Vladimir Komarov, Konstantin Feoktistov and Boris Yegorov. Their mission lasted 24 hours, 17 minutes. Later reports revealed that Feoktistov and Yegorov suffered from space sickness throughout the mission.

Touted as "the world's first space laboratory," Voskhod carried the first scientists into space. Feoktistov was a member of Korolev's engineering team and Yegorov was a physician specializing in aviation medicine and the effects of weightlessness on balance and the inner ear. During their flight they performed various tests aimed at discovering the effects of weightlessness and spaceflight on human physiology and performance.

Komorov, Feoktistov and Yegorov were also the first to travel in space without the protection of space suits in case the cabin depressurized, and, unlike the Vostok cosmonauts, they landed inside their spacecraft—

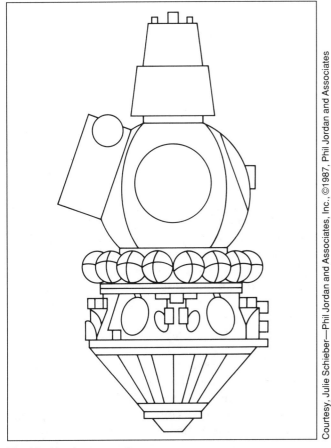

The Voskhod spacecraft

Courtesy, Julie Schieber—Phil Jordan and Associates, Inc., ©1987, Phil Jordan and Associates

requiring development of a new soft-landing system. As a result, their safe landing on the plains of Kazakhstan on October 13 was greeted by an enormous sigh of relief by Korolev, his engineers and the Soviet space team.

Meanwhile, although Khrushchev had chatted with the cosmonauts during their one-day trip, by the time they returned to Earth, Khrushchev's regime had been suddenly replaced in a power play by Leonid Brezhnev. The cosmonauts' arrival in Moscow shortly afterward was greeted by a new set of leaders.

Voskhod 2: One Man Outside a Spaceship

The Soviets followed up the three-man flight with still another impressive first. On March 18, 1965, they launched Voskhod 2, carrying two cosmonauts, Pavel Belyayev and Alexei Leonov—this time in space suits—and during their flight of 26 hours and two minutes, Leonov became the first human being ever to take a walk in space outside his spacecraft.

The enormous courage of the first human being who ever stepped out of a spacecraft to go it alone cannot be overestimated. Few have ever taken on a challenge with so many unknown consequences, and few have had the chance to make such a momentous impact on the place of humankind in the universe.

The Voskhod Spacecraft

Country: USSR

Crew: Two to three

Modules: Two, a reentry capsule and an equipment module

Versions: Two, one for three-man crew; the other for EVA

Diameter: Reentry capsule—7.2 ft. (2.2m)

Weight: Reentry capsule—5,291 lb. (2,400 kg)

EVA Airlock: 6 ft. (2m) long, 3 ft. (1m) diameter

The Voskhod spacecraft, as far as we know, was a Vostok slightly modified by chief designer Sergei Korolev and his team for flying a three-man crew and for use in a space walk (EVA or extravehicular activity)

demonstration. The ejection seats were replaced by smaller couches and a third one was placed slightly forward of the other two for the Voskhod 1 flight. In Voskhod 2, the third couch was removed to make room for the space suit used by Alexei Leonov in his EVA.

The spherical reentry capsule, containing the crew cabin, sat atop a service compartment that contained instrumentation, retro-rockets and batteries. The service module was jettisoned immediately after firing the retro-rockets before reentry. Unlike the Vostok, however, the Voskhod was designed to make a soft landing with the crew inside.

Records set by Voskhod missions included the first three-man crew in space, the first physician in space, the first orbit without space suits and the first EVA. Due to a malfunction, Voskhod 2 also performed the first Soviet manual reentry.

Voskhod 2 was especially modified with an inflatable decompression tunnel, or airlock, for Leonov's historic space walk (EVA). Once in orbit, the decompression chamber was extended outside a special EVA hatch. Air was pumped into it, making it possible for Leonov, with his space suit on, to enter and adapt to lowered and finally zero pressure before emerging into the vacuum of space. After the EVA, he reversed the process to readapt to pressurized atmosphere before reentering the cabin. Once the cosmonauts were on their way home, the EVA tunnel was jettisoned.

Voskhod spacecraft made a total of four missions, two of them unmanned and designated Cosmos 47 and 57. Voskhod was the last spacecraft that Korolev would see to its completion.

Working in the cabin's pure oxygen environment (used instead of the cosmonauts' usual oxygen-nitrogen, to keep Leonov from getting "the bends"), Leonov opened the Voskhod cabin hatch as the spacecraft passed in its second orbit above the Soviet Union. He eased himself into the special extravehicular activity (EVA) airlock that was by now extended from the Voskhod capsule and also filled with oxygen. Once inside the cramped 3-foot (1-m) diameter, 6-foot-long (2-m) cylinder, with the hatch

Alexei Leonov works out in preparation for his historic space walk

closed behind him, he inflated his suit and depressurized the airlock. A few moments later, he opened the outside hatch and looked out onto a sea of bright, unblinking stars "the color of red-gold." "A fantastic sight!" he would later describe the view. "The stars appeared to be motionless. The sun . . . seemed as if sewn onto black velvet. In the universe only one thing moved and that was Earth." Below he could see the dark waters of the Black Sea and the Caucasian coastline.

With the announcement, "I'm pushing off," Leonov glided out away from the Voskhod on a 16-foot (4.88-m) tether, spinning rapidly in response to his push with nothing to stop his movement. Millions at home watched on TV as he floated, arms stretched out, and exclaimed, "Man has walked out into space!" Breathing oxygen from a pack on his back, he kept in communication with both Earth and the spacecraft through his tether, which also carried an emergency oxygen line and data lines to report his vital signs to ground control.

All went well until, at the end of his 10 minutes of somersaults and pushoffs, it was time for Leonov to get back into the Voskhod airlock. The space suit ballooned from the pressure inside it, was stiff and awkward to move in, and getting back into the spacecraft turned out to be no easy matter. When Leonov tried to put the TV camera he had used to record his historic walk inside the airlock, it kept floating out, and his pulse raced up to a high 168, twice the normal rate, as he struggled to squeeze back in through the open airlock hatch. He finally succeeded—but lack of foot restraints for leverage had made it a major effort!

Once back inside Voskhod, the job of the mission accomplished, Belyayev and Leonov jettisoned the EVA airlock and prepared for reentry. But more bad news was in the works: part of the automatic reentry system had failed and they would have to return on manual pilot—a job never before performed by a Soviet cosmonaut. After missing their first reentry opportunity (something like missing your exit on the freeway), the calm, cool Belyayev brought them down without a hitch, though about 1,200 miles (2,000 km) off-course, in the snow-covered Ural mountains, far from their rescue teams. They spent a long, cold night hiding from hungry wolves inside their Voskhod capsule. Help arrived the next morning, however, and they were whisked off to the nearby town of Perm and eventually back to the cosmodrome at Tyuratam.

A talented artist, Leonov would later share what he had seen in space, not just in words, but through his paintings and drawings as well.

Ten months after Belyayev and Leonov's impressive flight, chief designer Sergei Korolev was dead at the age of 60. His health weakened by his years of imprisonment under the Stalin regime, he died during heart surgery on January 14, 1966. Only after his death was his identity made public (he had always been referred to as "the chief designer" in news reports). Now, at the time of his death, his contribution was openly appreciated, and his ashes, like those of other Soviet heroes, were placed in the Kremlin Wall in Moscow. Nikita Khrushchev wrote later in his memoirs, "I'm only sorry that we didn't manage to send a man to the Moon during Korolev's lifetime." It took many years for the Soviet space program to recover from his loss.

Gemini: Flying Two Astronauts

Meanwhile, in a speech to the U.S. Congress on May 25, 1961, just 20 days after Alan Shepard's historic Mercury flight in "Freedom 7," President John F. Kennedy had set his famous challenge: "I believe that this nation should commit itself to achieving the goal, before this decade is out, of landing a man on the Moon and returning him safely to the Earth." Meeting that challenge would take more technical expertise and more rocket power than either the U.S. or the USSR had developed at that time. The little Mercury capsule wasn't capable of the long, arduous flight to the Moon, either. Getting there was a big project and it would take two separate spacecraft development programs—Gemini and Apollo—to do the job.

Gemini 3: The Program Begins

Affectionately called the "Gus-mobile" (after Virgil "Gus" Grissom, the first mission commander), the Gemini ("Twins") capsule offered a tight squeeze for its two-man crew—something like sitting sideways in a phone booth. Following two unmanned Gemini tests in April 1964 and January 1965, the first manned Gemini flight was launched on March 23, with Grissom and John Young aboard, five days after the launch

From left to right are: Commander of the spaceship Voskhod Col. Vladimir Komarov, physician Boris Yegorov, and scientist Konstantin Feoktistov.

Gemini capsule at McDonnell Douglas plant in St. Louis

Courtesy, McDonnell Douglass

of Voskhod 2. They made a total of three orbits, and the flight lasted four hours and 53 minutes.

Grissom, who had almost drowned in the loss of the Liberty Bell 7 Mercury capsule, had named Gemini 3 Molly Brown, after the "Unsinkable Molly Brown" of the popular musical. Grissom and Young were the first crew to use the new system for maneuvering the spacecraft in orbit and they were also the first to eat a corned-beef sandwich in space, which Young had smuggled onboard.

On the way back down to Earth Grissom and Young found they had to correct for some miscalculations in Gemini's aerodynamics (the way it was affected by air flow), but reentry went smoothly except for a sudden jolt when the main parachute opened, smashing the astronauts against the window. After splashdown they were greeted by a jubilant reception committee aboard the aircraft carrier *Intrepid*, followed by commendation by President Lyndon Johnson and a ticker-tape parade in New York. America had taken its first step on the long trip to the Moon.

Gemini 4: U.S. Tries Spacewalking

With Leonov's space walk in March, the USSR had thrown down the gauntlet, and NASA had decided immediately afterward to take up the challenge and give spacewalking a try much earlier than originally planned. Less than three months after the Gemini 3 mission, on June 3, the U.S. launched Gemini 4 with astronauts Ed White and James McDivitt aboard. The two-day flight was to be not only the longest U.S. spaceflight to date, but also the occasion of the first U.S. space walk. Originally the plan had called for White just to extend head and shoulders from the spacecraft, but, following Leonov's success, the plan became more ambitious.

The Gemini Spacecraft

Country: U.S.

Crew: 2

Modules: 2—Reentry Module (command module) and Service Module (Titan capsule-rocket adaptor section)

Weight: 8,157 lb. (3,700 kg), overall; 5,952 lb. (2,700 kg), command module in orbit; 2,205 lb (1,000 kg), service module in orbit

Height: 11 ft. (3.35 m)

Diameter: (at base) 7.7 ft. (2.35 m)

Before landing a human on the surface of the Moon, there was still a lot NASA needed to know about maneuvering a spacecraft in orbit, rendezvousing with another spacecraft, and working in space outside a vehicle. The Gemini program was designed as a stepping stone; its job was to develop those areas before going on to the Apollo missions to the Moon.

Bell-shaped like the Mercury spacecraft, Gemini was larger overall and weighed 172% more. Yet the cabin space allotted to each crew member inside was actually reduced from 55 to 40 cubic feet (1.56 to 1.13 cu m). The Gemini spacecraft consisted of two main modules, the reentry or command module and the service or rocket-capsule adaptor module.

The reentry module, in turn, was composed of three parts: a cylinder-shaped nose for docking in orbit (and which also contained the descent parachute), a section containing attitude control engines (16 jets in two independent systems) and the crew cabin at the rear. Pressurized with 100 percent oxygen, the crew cabin contained side-by-side ejection seats for the two crew members. No safety tower was used on the Gemini since the seats were designed to eject crew members from the capsule in the event of an emergency.

The unpressurized adaptor section, aft of the cabin, consisted of two sections: an area housing retro-rockets for use in reentry to the Earth's atmosphere from orbit and another for housing equipment and fuel. This equipment section, located at the extreme rear of the spacecraft, had a special gold-covered shield to protect its contents from radiation and reflect sunlight. The Gemini link-up with the second stage of the Titan 2 rocket was also located at the rear. The spacecraft jettisoned both service sections before entering the atmosphere.

"Firsts" aboard Gemini included the first U.S. space walk (by Edward White on Gemini 4), the first U.S. rendezvous of spacecraft to spacecraft (Gemini 6 and 7) and the first manned docking (Gemini 8, with an Agena target vehicle).

Because the Atlas launcher that had boosted the Mercury capsules into orbit didn't have the power to launch the 8,000-pound (3,500-kg) Gemini, NASA used a modified two-stage Titan intercontinental ballistic missile.

Like the Mercury capsules, the 13 Gemini capsules were built by McDonnell in St. Louis. The first manned mission took place on March 23, 1965, with Virgil "Gus" Grissom and John Young completing three Earth orbits in Gemini 3.

After partially depressurizing the cabin, a check was made to make sure the astronauts' space suits were holding pressure. (On Earth we live at the bottom of a deep layer of atmosphere, which presses down on us. Our bodies are made to live in this atmospheric pressure, and without it we couldn't breathe and our organs would burst open. In the vacuum of space, where there is no air—no oxygen and no pressure—and no warmth, we can't live, even for a moment without using pressurized, temperature-regulated suits and an oxygen supply.) After expelling the rest of the oxygen from the cabin, White and McDivitt waited for a go-ahead from the ground as they passed over Hawaii. It came, and Ed White stood up and poked his head out.

McDivitt and the world waited restlessly, while White insisted on checking the lens cap on his 16 mm camera three times before going any further. ("I knew I might as well not come back," he later explained, if a forgotten lens cap got in the way of recording the historic occasion!) After putting together a small hand-held gas gun that he could use to propel himself in space—12 long minutes after the hatch had opened—White was ready to begin his space walk.

Using the gun as he floated out of the rectangular Gemini hatch, White moved away from the spacecraft and then made a somersault past its nose. He pulled on the long, gold-covered tether that carried oxygen, communication and power lines to his space suit (he had a nine-minute emergency oxygen supply in a chest unit). The pull sent him over the spacecraft toward its rear. Another blast from his gun propelled him back toward the nose between the two hatches and then he stabilized by shooting in the opposite direction. After only four minutes, however, the gun ran out of air, and White now had to maneuver solely by using the tether, just as Leonov had done.

Like Leonov, White took his space walk over his homeland and could pick out the familiar outline of Hawaii, California, Texas, Florida, the Bahamas and Bermuda below as he somersaulted above them. Using only the tether, White reeled and bounced a bit now, gently bumping against the spacecraft skin at one point, while McDivitt found that keeping Gemini steady with all that activity going on outside wasn't easy. He was, however, able to take some stunning photos of White through the window.

After 21 minutes, White got the signal from Houston to come back in. He had nearly doubled Leonov's extravehicular activity (EVA) time. After an exertion of effort that sent White's heart rate racing to 180, White and McDivitt secured the hatch, a step crucial to their survival on reentry. The total time—from the moment the hatch opened to the moment it closed at the end of the space walk—had taken a total of 36 minutes.

NASA

Ed White takes a space walk on June 3, 1965, during Gemini 4 mission. Note the maneuvering gun he holds in his hand

For the remainder of the mission White and Mc-Divitt took photographs, performed exercises and completed a total of 11 scientific experiments, more than had ever been completed on any previous spaceflight. After 62 orbits taking 97 hours and 56 minutes of flight time, the spacecraft splashed down on June 7. The mission was a huge success.

Gemini 5: The Garbage Can

By now the U.S. was ready to try longer missions to test whether humans could travel as far as the Moon. Gordon Cooper and Charles "Pete" Conrad, aboard Gemini 5, spent eight days in space— twice the length of the previous mission. The consensus: Humans could live in weightlessness long enough to go to the Moon, visit and come back. Of course, living in space that long wasn't guaranteed to be pleasant (Conrad jokingly referred to the mission as "eight days in a garbage can.") In fact, garbage was an annoyance throughout the Gemini missions. James Lovell of

Gemini 7 remarked that with all the garbage he and Frank Borman had stashed away by the end of their mission there would be no room left for the crew!

Gemini 5 performed a successful simulated rendezvous and the crew completed 16 of the 17 experiments planned. They also released the first satellite launched from a spacecraft. Cooper and Conrad returned to Earth on August 29 in excellent physical condition. "There was absolutely nothing wrong with them," according to the medical report.

Gemini 6 and 7: Double Twins

Gemini 6, which was originally scheduled to perform a rendezvous and docking exercise using an Agena vehicle (see box on the Agena Target Vehicle) as the target, did not launch as planned on October 25. The Agena, which was launched first, would enter orbit, where the Gemini crew could meet it (rendezvous) in their craft and dock with it. This time, however, the Agena apparently exploded before it ever got there.

As a result, the next Gemini crew to fly was the Gemini 7 crew, consisting of Frank Borman and James Lovell, launched on December 4, 1965. They made 220 revolutions in 330 hours and 35 minutes, a total of two weeks, establishing a duration record that would stand for five years. Unlike McDivitt on Gemini 4, Borman succeeded in station-keeping in a rendezvous exercise with the spent second stage of the launch rocket.

On December 15, after several delays, Gemini 7 was joined in space by Walter Schirra and Thomas Stafford aboard Gemini 6 (now officially called Gemini 6A). With Gemini 7 acting as the target, Schirra maneuvered his spacecraft within 6 feet (2 m) of the aircraft and, speeding above the Earth at 17,500 mph (28,000 kmh), Schirra "kept station," hovering nearby for 5 1/2 hours. At one point, according to some sources, Schirra carefully nosed in to a distance of only 1 foot (.30 m), without touching. "Hello there. What kept you?" the Gemini 7 astronauts jibed delightedly. Later, as the two spacecraft backed off to safe orbits for the night, someone aboard Gemini 7 remarked warmly, "We have company tonight."

Gemini 6 splashed down the next day on December 16, followed two days later by Gemini 7 on December 18. The first close rendezvous between two spacecraft with humans aboard had succeeded.

Gemini 8: The Spacecraft That Docked

Neil Armstrong and David Scott, launched aboard Gemini 8 on March 16, 1966, became the first to dock

NASA

View of Gemini 7 from Gemini 6 during rendezvous

the Gemini 8 spacecraft itself! After several frightening moments it became apparent that one of the craft's thrusters (or rockets) was firing out of control. The crew shut down the system for maneuvering the spacecraft in order to quiet the problem thruster. Then they reactivated reentry control to stop the tumbling of the spacecraft. Almost 75 percent of the fuel had been depleted through the thruster, and the rest of the mission was immediately scrapped. Armstrong and Scott made the first Gemini landing in the Pacific on March 17.

Gemini 9: More Trouble

Sometimes called a bad-luck mission, Gemini 9 had a troubled history before even getting off the ground. The astronauts originally assigned to fly Gemini 9, Elliott See and Charles Bassett, died in training on February 28, 1966, as they tried to land a jet in bad weather at the McDonnell factory in St. Louis where the Gemini spacecraft were built. Three months later, backup crew Tom Stafford and Eugene Cernan had to abandon their scheduled launch on May 17 when the Agena satellite, launched that day, failed to orbit.

The mission was finally launched, however, on June 3 with Stafford and Cernan aboard (under the official designation Gemini 9A). Their mission lasted 44 revolutions and a total of 72 hours, 21 minutes, but the docking phase was still disappointing when a protective covering or shroud over their target's docking adaptor failed to clear away and they couldn't dock.

An EVA by Cernan didn't go exactly according to plan, either. Scheduled to perform a space walk lasting two and one-half hours, Cernan was supposed to go to Gemini's adaptor section, put on a backpack propulsion unit that was stored there, and propel himself out into space, still tethered to the spacecraft.

However, it didn't work out quite that way. Unaware of Leonov's scare aboard Voskhod 2, Cernan ran into a problem putting the backpack on because he couldn't hold steady. Every movement propelled him in another, often unwanted, direction. In his struggle he became overheated, his pulse rate racing as high as 180, and his visor fogged up so he was unable to see. Finally, recognizing the danger of continuing his space walk with his vision so clouded, the astronaut finally abandoned the rest of the EVA, left the backpack in the adaptor and returned to the safety of the spacecraft. He had, however, performed a record-breaking space walk of two hours, eight minutes, even though he hadn't accomplished everything he had set out to.

one spacecraft with another in space. Just a little over six hours into their mission, they eased in to a distance of 2 feet (.60 m) from their Agena target, which was also launched March 16. They received a go-ahead from the tracking ship below and pulled the Gemini's cone into the adaptor at one end of the Agena's docking adaptor that made docking possible. The latches snapped in place to fasten the two spacecraft firmly together.

Dubbed "a smoothie" by Armstrong, the docking seemed to have gone perfectly, when Scott noticed a yawing (shift to one side) and the two joined spacecraft began to buck ominously. Concerned that the docking assembly might give way under the stress, Armstrong backed away from the Agena, but the bucking only got worse. The problem was clearly in

NASA

Astronauts Neil Armstrong and David Scott could see the gentle curve of the Earth from their Gemini 8 spacecraft as they rendezvoused with their Agena target at a distance of 210 feet on March 16, 1966

Despite its problems, Gemini 9 splashed down on June 6 only 0.50 miles (0.80 km) from the recovery ship.

Gemini 10: Double Agena

Gemini 10, scheduled to fly only six weeks later, picked up where Gemini 9 had left off. John Young and Michael Collins, launched on July 18, made a brief three-day flight (70 hours, 47 minutes) of 43 revolutions. In that short time Gemini 10 made two rendezvous.

First, Gemini docked with an Agena target (Gemini Target Vehicle [GTV] 10), launched the same day. Young then fired the Agena's engine to boost the two docked vehicles into a 473-mile (761-km) orbit, a record.

Later, Young separated Gemini 10 from GTV 10 to rendezvous the spacecraft with GTV 8, the Agena target used by Gemini 8 and left in orbit. Once docked, Collins set out on the major space walk of the mission. At the end of a 50-foot (15-m) tether, in the first spacecraft-to-spacecraft EVA, Collins used a nitrogen gun to propel himself across to GTV 8 to collect a micrometeoroid experiment. When the Agena began to tumble as Collins bumped into it, the two astronauts decided to cut the EVA short.

During the mission, the astronauts opened the hatch three times, but two EVAs were cut short. A standup EVA photographing stars and the colors of space was ended after about 50 minutes because of unexplained fumes that caused the two astronauts' eyes to water so badly they could hardly see.

Gemini 10 splashed down on July 21 in the Atlantic Ocean just four miles from the recovery ship.

Gemini 11: Emergency Dry-Run

On September 12, 1966, astronauts Pete Conrad and Richard Gordon set a record in a docking tour-de-force. Launched aboard Gemini 11, they rendezvoused and docked with their Agena target on the first

---

The Agena Target Vehicle

Country: U.S.

Crew: None

Weight: 1,698 lb. (770 kg)

Length: 23.3 ft. (7.1 m)

Diameter: 4.9 ft. (1.5 m)

Main Propulsion: Bell rocket engine with a thrust of 15,432 lb. (7,000 kg)

Agena upper-stage rockets became an important part of the Gemini program because of their ability to be placed accurately into orbit, to reignite and change orbit and to be maneuvered precisely. Launched atop Atlas rockets, they were used as target vehicles for rendezvous, docking and/or maneuvering exercises in five Gemini missions.

At one end of the cylindrical vehicle, a rendezvous cone and "V" seat made it possible for an orbiting Gemini spacecraft to be guided into place and then locked into the Agena to make a two-part spacecraft (first accomplished by Gemini 8). As Gemini missions became more sophisticated, the Agena's propulsion system and attitude-control thrusters were powered up and controlled from the docked Gemini craft to change orbit and execute maneuvers (first accomplished by Gemini 10).

A secondary propulsion system consisted of two 16-pound (7.3-kg) rockets and two 199.7-lb. (90.6 kg) rockets.

In well over 300 launches, only some 30 Agena rockets have failed. Produced by Lockheed Missiles and Space Company, the Agena has been used extensively for launching satellites, especially by the military, and first came into use in 1959.

---

revolution around the Earth, just one hour and 34 minutes into the flight. They relied only on their onboard computer and radar equipment and effectively showed that astronauts on the Moon's surface could launch and dock speedily with a Command Module for an emergency return to Earth if necessary. In experiments that followed, both Conrad and Gordon docked and undocked the Gemini spacecraft with the Agena.

In one EVA attempt, Gordon floated out the opened hatch to attach a 100-foot (30-m) tether to the docked Agena for a series of experiments, but he didn't succeed in making the connection on the first try. After being reeled in by Conrad, he went back out and straddled the Gemini nose to free his hands—to an encouraging shout of "Ride 'em, cowboy!" from Conrad. Success came hard, though—manipulating in weightlessness was much more difficult than in training on Earth—and Gordon's eyes became blinded with sweat. Finally Conrad called him back in after just 33 minutes with the hatch open.

With the two craft docked, they burned the Agena engines and the combined vehicle soared to a new record of 850 miles (1,373 km), where Conrad and Gordon became the first humans to see the roundness of Earth's surface. At a lower orbit Gordon took photographs during a standup EVA that lasted two hours and 41 minutes.

This was followed, however, by one of the mission's most exciting experiments. After undocking from the Agena, the crew manipulated their spacecraft out to the opposite end of the tether between the two craft. At first, the two units moved independently in space, the tether looping between them in what Conrad described as a wild, "rope-skipping" movement. As Conrad let the two craft find their own positions, however, the line drew taut between them. In maneuvers that followed, Conrad and Gordon experienced the first "artificial gravity" (though very slight) created experimentally by two rotating tethered spacecraft, which pulled against each other to create a force that felt like a weaker form of Earth's gravity.

After further maneuvers, the Gemini 11 crew finally said good-bye to the Agena, which they claimed was "the best friend we ever had." The Gemini 11 mission had lasted 44 revolutions, taking two days, 23 hours, and 17 minutes. The crew made a computer-controlled reentry (the first for an American spacecraft), splashing down in the Atlantic on September 15.

Astronauts Tom Stafford and Gene Cernan met with disappointment aboard Gemini 9 when they couldn't dock with their target. Mocking them like giant alligator jaws, the protective shroud on the docking adaptor failed to drop away as it was supposed to and blocked access as they sped high above the Earth's clouds and oceans.

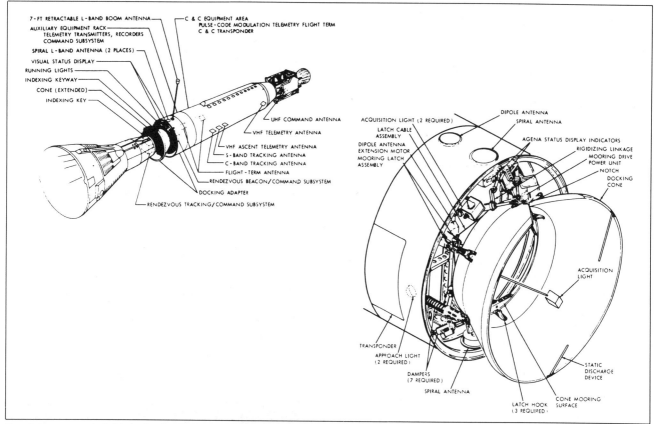

Gemini spacecraft (left) docked with Agena target   Agena's docking section

Gemini 12: The Final Mission

At one time the Gemini program's final launch had been slated for a dual Gemini-Apollo mission, but by the end of 1966, Apollo 1 was still not ready to go. So James Lovell and Edwin "Buzz" Aldrin blasted off on November 11, 1966, without Apollo, for the last Gemini mission. Even though its radar system to aid seeking out a target had gone out, like previous Gemini missions, Gemini 12 docked quickly and efficiently with its Agena satellite target (launched the same day as Gemini). The crew also had a chance to photograph a solar eclipse from space.

The main objective of the mission, though, was to evaluate the range of activity that could be performed during EVA. Aldrin spent a total of five and one-half hours in three outings, the first completely successful space walks. The first lasted two hours, 29 minutes, but it was limited. Aldrin just stood up on his couch with the hatch open, only his head and shoulders protruding. While Lovell quipped, "What did I tell you? Four days' vacation and see the world," Aldrin was dazzled by the view. Not too dazzled, though, to

do his job—performing numerous tasks, taking photographs and installing a handrail to be used later.

The next day in another EVA, Aldrin navigated toward the nose of the Gemini craft, using the handrail he had installed, and tried out various gadgets developed to solve some of the problems other spacewalkers had experienced. To free his hands, he could hook nylon tethers from his waist onto the handrail or rings on the Agena, as well as a batch of portable Velcro handholds that could be attached to special areas of the spacecraft. He also tried out an overshoe-like foot restraint attached to the rear of the craft, which he found worked beautifully. After connecting the Gemini and the Agena with a tether, Aldrin pioneered the idea of astronaut/repair man by testing his ability to screw and unscrew bolts and manipulate connectors while he floated weightless at a workstation aboard Agena. Unlike other Gemini spacewalkers, Aldrin had no trouble with overheating, in subdued light or daylight, his visor didn't fog and his pulse rate remained as low as 120. The two-hour, eight-minute space walk was a resounding success.

The astronauts performed 14 scientific experiments, more artificial gravity tests and one more stand-up EVA. After a fully automatic reentry, Gemini 12 returned to Earth on November 15. The flight had lasted three days, 22 hours, 34 minutes.

The last mission complete, Gemini had done its job. It had given the U.S. nearly 2,000 human hours in space, plus experience with working in space, rendezvous, docking and landing from orbit. Learning how to rendezvous, or meet, with another spacecraft would be crucial to the upcoming Moon missions, since (amid considerable controversy) the decision was made to use what NASA called a Lunar Orbital Rendezvous, a process that would be simpler than trying to land a big rocket on the Moon. The idea was to put the main Apollo spacecraft (Command Module or CM) in orbit and send a small vehicle (Lunar Module or LM) down to land on the Moon. It would later return from the surface to lunar orbit to meet back up with the Command Module and the astronauts would transfer back to the CM and return to Earth.

Over the course of 10 manned missions, the maneuverable Gemini spacecraft had shown that people could live in space as long as two weeks (more than long enough to go to the Moon and back), that we could launch two astronauts in the same spacecraft, that humans could accomplish tasks during space walks and that rendezvous and docking were achievable goals—all necessary precursors to meeting Kennedy's 1961 challenge to "fly man to the Moon in this decade." For the first time, its astronauts were true spacecraft pilots, aided by an onboard computer and powered by rockets for maneuvering in space. Most of all, the U.S. had gained the confidence to fly to the Moon.

Milestones In Space: The Gemini and Voskhod Years, 1964-1966

1964   January 29: U.S. Saturn SA-5 sends a record 19 tons into orbit

April 8: U.S. Gemini 1 orbits for four days in an unmanned orbital test

July 28: U.S. launches Ranger 7, which sends back 4,300 close-up images of the Moon

October 12: Voskhod 1 makes the first multi-person spaceflight, with Soviet cosmonauts Vladimir Komarov, Boris Yegorov, and Konstantin Feoktistov aboard

1965   January 19: U.S. runs an unmanned 18-minute suborbital test of the Gemini 2 heat shield

March 18: Soviet cosmonaut Alexei Leonov completes the first extravehicular activity (EVA) or space walk, when he floats for 10 minutes outside his Voskhod 2 spacecraft

March 23: U.S. Gemini 3 makes the first manned flight of Project Gemini with "Gus" Grissom and John Young on board, and carrying a computer to enable the astronauts to truly pilot the spacecraft

April 6: Communications satellite "Early Bird" (Intelsat I) becomes the first commercial satellite to be launched into geostationary orbit

June 3: Ed White makes the first American EVA in a 21-minute maneuver. Aloft for 4 days, he and James McDivitt make 62 orbits in Gemini 4

July 14: U.S. spacecraft Mariner 4 flies within 6,118 miles (9,846 km) of Mars after an eight-month journey for the first close-up images of "the Red Planet." (Launched November 28, 1964)

August 21: U.S. astronauts Gordon Cooper and "Pete" Conrad set a new international record with an eight-day, 120-orbit trip around Earth aboard Gemini 5

December 4: Gemini 7, flown by Frank Borman and Jim Lovell, makes a 14-day flight setting an international long-duration record that holds for 5 years until Russia's 18-day Soyuz 9 flight in 1970

December 15: U.S. astronauts Wally Schirra and Tom Stafford complete the first true space rendezvous, flying Gemini 6-A within a few feet of Gemini 7, which is already in orbit

1966   February 3: Soviet Moon lander Luna 9 drops onto the Ocean of Storms and returns the first photographs from the lunar surface. (Launched January 31)

February 28: Charles Bassett and Elliott See, scheduled to fly Gemini 9 in May, are both killed in a jet airplane accident in St. Louis

March 1: The Soviet Venera 3 spacecraft crash lands on Venus, becoming the first human-made object to land on another planet. (Launched November 16, 1965)

March 16: In the world's first docking of two spacecraft, U.S. astronauts Neil Armstrong and Dave Scott link Gemini 8 up with an orbiting Agena target vehicle, perform an EVA, and make a safe emergency landing after the two linked craft spin out of control

April 3: The Soviet spacecraft Luna 10 becomes the first to achieve Lunar orbit. (Launched March 31)

June 2: Surveyor 1, the first American spacecraft to soft-land on the Moon, touches down on the Ocean of Storms. (Launched May 30)

June 3: Gemini 9 back-up crew Tom Stafford and Eugene Cernan make this much-postponed U.S. flight, featuring a 2-hour EVA by Cernan and a near-perfect splashdown

July 18: Two successful rendezvous and docking maneuvers with Agena targets, plus EVAs by Mike Collins, mark the U.S. Gemini 10 mission, flown by Collins and John Young

September 12: Pete Conrad and Richard Gordon fly Gemini 11 to rendezvous and dock with their Agena target in one hour, 34 minutes from launch time. Two EVAs and a high orbit of 850 miles (1,373 km) with the Agena were also achieved, along with preliminary artificial gravity experiments

November 11: Gemini 12, flown by Jim Lovell and Buzz Aldrin, becomes the last mission flown by U.S. Project Gemini. The mission includes three highly successful EVAs (the first fully successful ones), docking with an Agena target, artificial-gravity experiments and a fully automatic reentry

9

1967: A BAD YEAR FOR SPACE

*H*ow do you expect to get us to the Moon if you people can't even hook us up with a ground station?

Gus Grissom, during the last test of the Apollo 1 spacecraft

In the U.S. the last Gemini flight had gone through its paces, the technology was working, and hopes ran high for the Apollo program in early 1967 as time for the first manned launch approached. Gus Grissom, veteran of both the Mercury and Gemini programs, would command the first flight, a 14-day test run set for February 21. Ed White, the first American to walk in space, and rookie Roger Chaffee had been chosen to complete the crew.

Behind the scenes, however, not all was going smoothly with the development of the Apollo Command Service Module (CSM), the main spacecraft of the program. As NASA began to put the craft through pre-flight tests in late 1966, problem after problem turned up. A transistor failed. The oxygen regulator in the environmental control system failed. The fuel tank design came under scrutiny when a similar fuel tank ruptured. The new environmental control system leaked and spilled liquid coolant across electrical wiring. Many minor defects were revealed. As a result, the project saw delay after delay while engineers struggled to fix the problems. Disappointed with the way the spacecraft was coming together, Grissom hung a lemon on its hatch one day in what turned out to be a grim symbol of the CSM's shortcomings.

Finally mated to the Saturn IB rocket that was scheduled to put it into Earth orbit, Apollo 1 was ready for a dry run of the countdown. The rocket held no fuel and no ignition would be touched off, but otherwise the test held on January 27, 1967, was to be a simulation of an actual launch. The crew had taken their places, strapped side by side onto their couches inside the cabin. The hatch was closed and locked. The atmosphere inside was 100 percent oxygen at normal pressure—16 pounds per square inch. It was 6:31 P.M. Interrupted all afternoon with various problems, the countdown had stopped once again, at T minus 10, to allow work on a troublesome intercom.

That's when the unthinkable happened. A short in the wiring sent a spark into the pure-oxygen environment of the capsule, and in a matter of seconds the crew was engulfed in an inferno of flame. Just 10 seconds after the short occurred Roger Chaffee reported the fire over the intercom: "We've got a bad fire—let's get out . . . We're burning up!" In the following seconds, Ed White leaped toward the hatch and began trying to get it open, but the unlatching procedure was too complex, the heat too searing and the smoke too suffocating. Hearing shouting and banging against the walls inside, the launch pad crew recognized the trouble and raced to try to unlock the

The charred interior of Apollo 1, January 27, 1967

hatch from the outside. An explosion and dense smoke sent them reeling back. Finally the hatch opened and one technician, in a heroic effort, managed to pull it away by himself. Four full minutes after the fire started, the fire detail arrived. They'd been on stand-by, but not on the scene because, with no fuel present, it had seemed an unnecessary precaution.

They were too late. Inside, the bodies of Grissom, Chaffee and White were charred and encased in molten nylon. Nylon netting extending across the ceiling to hold loose items in flight had provided the flames with a way to travel from one side to the other in a cabin that was supposed to be made entirely of inflammable material. The three astronauts had died of asphyxiation.

Grissom, a lieutenant colonel in the Air Force, and Chaffee, a Navy lieutenant commander, were both buried at Arlington Cemetery, while Lieutenant Colonel White was buried at West Point the same day.

The agonizing investigations that followed concluded that both NASA and North American Aviation, the CSM manufacturer, had overlooked dangerous hazards. The flammable netting should never have been used around pure oxygen, investigators said. The hatch shouldn't have been so hard to open (it required a minimum of 90 seconds). Before the investigators were finished they discovered numerous problems in workmanship, quality control and design, including a loose wrench socket left among the wiring.

The Apollo program had been moving too fast to be safe and now ground to a halt. Another 18 months would elapse while the spacecraft was redesigned to protect the safety of the Apollo astronauts who would fly the missions to come. The delay was worth the cost. By the time Apollo 7 took off, the crew was

surrounded by a virtually fireproofed cabin and the environment was a mix of nitrogen and oxygen on liftoff (replaced by pure oxygen only later in the flight). An escape valve could vent all the oxygen out of the cabin within a minute and the escape hatch took only 10 seconds to open.

Unfortunately, the Soviet Union was trying to move into space too fast as well. Pressure was intense to win in the race to the Moon, but the space program had been delayed waiting for the new Soyuz ("Union") spacecraft to be ready for use. By April 23, 1967, the Soviets were ready. Veteran cosmonaut Vladimir Komarov was launched into orbit at 3:35 A.M. Moscow time in the brand-new Soyuz 1 spacecraft. Many experts believed another cosmonaut crew—composed of Valery Bykovsky, Alexei Yeliseyev and Yevgeny Khrunov—would launch in a second Soyuz craft the next day. The two would dock in space and Yeliseyev and Khrunov would transfer to Soyuz 1 (a mission plan that was later executed by Soyuz 4 and 5). It would have been a natural follow-up to the Gemini rendezvous and docking successes of the previous two years.

Vladimir Komarov died when his Soyuz 1 capsule crashed to Earth on April 24, 1967

Early in the flight, however, Komarov's craft developed guidance problems. One of the two solar panels also failed to deploy, leaving Soyuz 1 underpowered. Komarov was in trouble and ground control decided to bring him down, but he missed the first opportunity to reenter and land, and ended up making an emergency descent, spinning like a bullet. Unable to stop the spinning and having no emergency ejection seat, Komarov plunged downward with his craft. The main parachute deployed, but became twisted and tangled in its lines by the spinning. With nothing to brake its spiraling fall to Earth, Soyuz 1 plummeted downward at several hundred miles per hour. Komarov's efforts to save himself were picked up over the radio by American ham operators listening in Norway until he crashed on the Orenburg steppe near the town of Novoorsk. Komarov was killed instantly, the first person to die during a space mission.

The Soviets, stunned by this first disaster in their space program, buried Komarov as a hero in the Kremlin Wall in Moscow.

The Soviet space program, like the Americans', would proceed soberly; design flaws in the Soyuz were carefully corrected over the coming 18 months. Yuri Gagarin (who would also die the following year in a jet plane crash) spoke for the spirit of exploration in all cosmonauts and astronauts—and all the rest of us—when he wrote these words about Komarov's death in 1967:

> Nothing will stop us. The road to the stars is steep and dangerous. But we're not afraid . . . Space flights can't be stopped. This isn't the work of one man or even a group of men. It is a historical process which mankind is carrying out in accordance with the natural laws of human development.

Profiles in Courage

Every astronaut or cosmonaut who has ventured into space from Yuri Gagarin onward has exhibited the ultimate in courage—the ability to face down the unknown and the all-too-possible prospect of death. When tragedy hit both programs in 1967, the very real risks of human exploration of space were clear to everyone. Roger Chaffee, Gus Grissom and Ed White in the U.S. and Vladimir Komarov in the USSR were not the first to die for this goal, nor would they be the last. But they were the first to die "on duty" and for that they are unique heroes of our time.

Roger Chaffee
February 15, 1935–January 26, 1967

No stranger to risk, Roger Bruce Chaffee was a lieutenant commander in the U.S. Navy, and as a Navy pilot attached to a Heavy Photographic Squadron he had flown numerous reconnaissance missions over Cuba in 1962 during the missile crisis when Americans spotted Soviet missiles on the big Carribean island off the coast of Florida. Selected for NASA's astronaut team with 13 others in 1963, he became a member of the Apollo 1 crew in March 1966 and, at 31, he was the youngest of the three. Apollo was to have been his first spaceflight.

Virgil "Gus" Grissom
April 3, 1926–January 26, 1967

Virgil Ivan Grissom, nicknamed Gus, was a veteran astronaut who had already taken his share of risks. As the astronaut aboard "Liberty Bell 7," the fourth Mercury program mission, he had nearly drowned in 1961 when the hatch blew off his capsule during splashdown in the Atlantic Ocean. Just under four years later, on March 23, 1965, as commander, he had pioneered the first Gemini spacecraft "Molly Brown" with John Young.

Even before coming to the space program, Grissom had shown his courage. As a member of the 75th Fighter Interceptor Squadron he had flown 100 combat missions during the war in Korea in 1950–1952. In May 1957 he had become a fighter test pilot at Wright-Patterson Air Force Base.

Fully aware that being an astronaut was risky business, just a few weeks before his death Grissom had written that, given the law of averages, the program would eventually lose somebody. When that happened, he added, "I hope the American people won't feel it's too high a price to pay for our space program."

As commander of the Apollo 1 mission, he would have been the first person to go into space three times and the first to fly three different spacecraft.

Edward White
November 14, 1930–January 26, 1967

Edward Higgins White II had also already shown a strong spirit of valor before coming to the Apollo program. A West Point graduate, during the Gemini 4 mission in June 1965 he had been the first American to venture into space wearing only a space suit to protect himself from the dangerous airless vacuum of space. White, too, had served as a test pilot at Wright-Patterson AFB before joining NASA and had logged over 4,200 hours of flying time. On Apollo 1 he would have scored another first—the first manned mission aboard the new spacecraft.

Vladimir Komarov
March 16, 1927–April 24, 1967

Dogged with health problems early in his career, Vladimir Mikhailovich Komarov had fought to stay in the cosmonaut program. He was a veteran of the three-cosmonaut Voskhod 1 mission, perhaps the most dangerous ever undertaken in space, which he had piloted in October 1964. With Soyuz 1, this crack pilot was at the helm of another new spacecraft. At age 40, Komarov was the oldest Soviet ever to fly in space as he set out on his Soyuz 1 flight on April 23, 1967. He was the first man to die during a mission to space.

10

SHOOTING FOR THE MOON: THE EARLY APOLLO YEARS, 1968–1969

The vast loneliness is awe-inspiring and it makes you realize just what you have back there on Earth. The Earth from here is a grand oasis in the big vastness of space.

—James Lovell, Apollo 8

While in 1961 it may have been easy enough to say "Let's go to the Moon," doing it was a complex undertaking. By 1968 the challenge had brought together people of diverse professions and expertise in a common effort to unlock the unknown and achieve the improbable.

The Saturn V Rocket

Country: U.S.

Height: 281.8 ft. (85.9 m)

Weight: 6.2 million lb. (2.8 million kg)

Overall Thrust: 8.855 million lb. (4.016 million kg) in three phases

Launch Capacity: 300,000 lb. (136,080 kg) to Earth orbit, or 100,000 lb (45,360 kg) to the Moon

Stages: 3 (lunar mission version)
  Stage 1, S-IC: Height, 138.1 ft. (42.1 m); Diameter, 32.8 ft. (10 m); Thrust, 7.5 million lb. (3.40 million kg)
  Stage 2, S-II: Height 81.4 ft (24.8 m); Diameter, 32.8 ft. (10 m); Thrust, 1.125 million lb. (510,300 kg)

Stage 3, S-IVB: Height, 59.4 ft. (18.1 m); Diameter, 21.7 ft. (6.6m); Thrust 230,004 lb. (104,328 kg)

Work on a giant rocket that could lift heavy loads to Earth orbit or even to the Moon began as early as 1959 under the visionary direction of Wernher von Braun, the German rocket pioneer who had come to the U.S. after World War II. Within two years von Braun began testing Saturn I, an early predecessor to the huge Saturn V rocket that would eventually go the the Moon.

Von Braun modified Saturn I to create a mid-range booster, called Saturn IB, which was used to launch early Apollo spacecraft into Earth orbit for testing. Three unmanned tests using the Saturn IB in 1966 went so well that hopes ran high for a manned test in early 1967. The Apollo 1 fire disaster, however, postponed that breakthrough.

But the giant Saturn V was ready to go, and it soon proved its mettle by carrying the unmanned Apollo 4 capsule into orbit on November 9, 1967. At lift-off, the five S-1 engines of the first stage—one fixed at the center and four clustered around it on gimbals—gave off a deafening roar that shook the ground. Five J-2 engines clustered in the same way came into play during the second-stage burn. The thundering power of the Saturn V knew no equal the world over.

The restartable J-2 engine of the third stage (which was the same as the Saturn IB's second stage) made it possible to park the Apollo in a temporary Earth orbit at 17,400 mph (28,000 km/h), then switch off and reignite to head towards the Moon.

From 1967 to 1972 the Saturn V launched a total of 12 Apollo missions—two unmanned test flights and 10 manned Apollo missions (one in Earth orbit, three around the Moon, and six Moon landings). In 1973 a 13th Saturn V put Skylab into orbit. Not once, with all of its millions of parts, did it fail. Manufactured by Boeing (first stage), Rockwell (second stage), Mc-Donnell Douglas (third stage), and Rocketdyne (engines), some Saturn V hardware remains—in mothballs—perhaps still usable for some giant job in the future that only a Saturn V can handle.

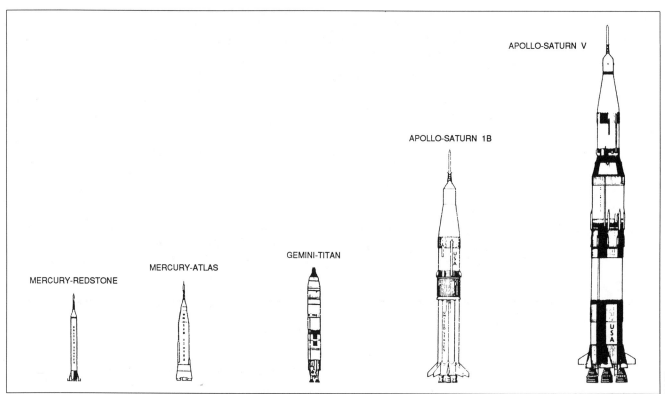

The Apollo program's Saturn V launcher was a giant compared to the Mercury and Gemini launch vehicles

Between 1961 and 1968, the U.S. sent a flock of unmanned missions to the Moon to find out more about our mysterious neighbor. What did the surface of the Moon look like from close up? Where could a spacecraft land safely? What was on the other side of the Moon? What was the consistency of the surface? Three programs tried to answer these questions so crucial to a manned landing: Ranger, Lunar Orbiter and Surveyor.

There was also a much bigger question these probes could help with, one which the Apollo program itself would attempt to answer: Where did the Moon come from? One of the Moon's great mysteries has always been its origin. Is it a "sister" planet, formed at the same time as the Earth? Was it torn away from the Earth by a passing comet or meteor? Or did the Earth pull it into its orbit as it passed through nearby space?

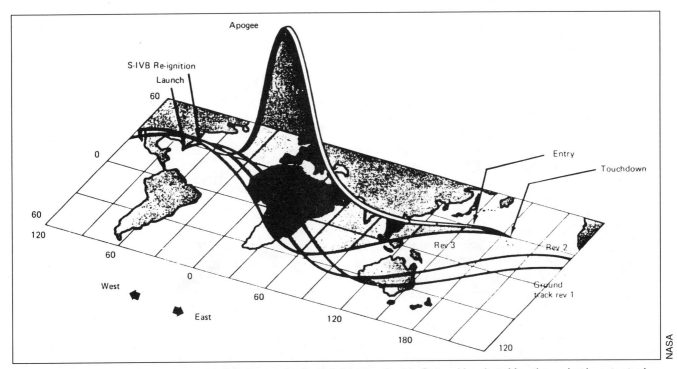

The flight path taken by the unmanned Apollo 4 test, the first craft to use the big Saturn V rocket. After the rocket booster took the Apollo 4 spacecraft upward to its peak, Apollo's own engine took over, accelerating the craft downward into the atmosphere to simulate reentry speed from a lunar flight.

From August 1961 to March 1965 a series of Ranger spacecraft were sent to land on the Moon, photographing as they approached its surface. Unfortunately, the missions had limited success. Of the nine missions launched, only the last three succeeded.

Beginning August 10, 1966, however, the U.S. sent five orbiting missions—dubbed the Lunar Orbiters—to map the entire surface of the Moon in a detailed reconnaissance study. In the process, the highly successful spacecraft responded to nearly 2,800 ground-based commands on a single mission and took thousands of photographs, including pictures of potential landing sites.

Meanwhile, between May 1966 and January 1968 the Surveyor program launched seven exploratory probes to land on the Moon. Five of them succeeded in making soft landings on the surface—a technology that would be vital to any manned mission to the Moon. They sent back valuable scientific and engineering data, including over 10,000 photographs from one mission alone, as well as surface analysis and extensive experimental data. In another first, Surveyor 6 also succeeded in lifting off from the moon's surface and moving 10 feet to a new location.

Apollo 7: At Last a Manned Test

As many recognized early, the project literally couldn't get off the ground without a mighty launch vehicle, a rocket of enormous power that could lift astronauts and spacecraft into Earth orbit and then escape the orbit to head for the Moon. By 1967 the Saturn V launcher was ready, its capability to lift heavy payloads away from Earth's gravity approaching 100 times that of the Redstone rocket that had launched Alan Shepard aboard Mercury in 1961. The giant rocket towered above all previous launchers in size, power and reliability, a tribute to technological accomplishment.

Three successful test launches of an unmanned spacecraft by a Saturn IB, a less powerful version of the Saturn V, had left planners optimistic in 1966 about scheduling a manned launch—until the Apollo 1 fire in January 1967. Stunned by the deaths of astronauts Grissom, White and Chaffee, NASA put all plans for a manned test on hold while engineers, designers and technicians went back to the drawing board to make the spacecraft safer for human travel.

As summer turned to fall in 1968, after two successful unmanned launches with the Saturn V (Apollo 4 and 6) and one with a Saturn IB (Apollo 5), at last the

Apollo Command Module looked ready to go. Launched on October 11, 1968, Wally Schirra, Donn Eisele and Walter Cunningham soared into Earth orbit atop a Saturn IB rocket as the nation watched anxiously on TV, the first time a space mission was broadcast. Their job: to put the Command/Service Module through its paces for the first time with a crew aboard.

As the mission progressed through it 11-day flight plan, ground observers breathed a sigh of relief at the lack of serious problems aboard the ship. Apollo was working the way it was supposed to. In a vital test of the spacecraft, the crew set off the explosive bolts to release the Command/Service Module (CSM) from the final stage of the Saturn rocket, the S-IVB. Once free, Schirra turned the CSM around front to rear to face the S-IVB, where the Lunar Module (LM) would ride in future flights (see box on Apollo spacecraft). Schirra succeeded in a rendezvous and station-keeping exercise about 100 feet away in this first test of the system—a procedure that would ultimately play a key role in the docking and transfer of astronauts to the LM for landing on the Moon.

Things went so smoothly, in fact, that the large margin of time allotted for solving unforeseen technical problems proved unnecessary. The ground crew began to introduce new, unplanned tests into the mission. Still haunted by the specter of the Apollo 1 fire and suffering from head colds, the three astronauts grew irritable. "We have a feeling you are believing that some of these experimenters are holier than God down there," Commander Schirra snapped at one point. "We are a heck of a lot closer to Him right now."

However, in seven live TV sessions—the first TV specials from space—the crew put on a good show despite their tension. Floating around their cabin, they performed acrobatics and cracked jokes in front of the tiny 4 1/2-pound black-and-white camera with messages like: "Hello from the lovely Apollo room high above everything." Their broadcasts were an enormous success.

Because of the head congestion caused by their colds, the three astronauts had to hold their noses and swallow during reentry to prevent rupturing their eardrums in the rapid descent. Just before they reentered the Earth's atmosphere on October 22, the Service Module retrofired its main engine as planned, then jettisoned, leaving the Command Module to descend by itself. Everything went perfectly until splashdown, when the capsule tipped over, briefly cutting off contact with the crew. It righted a few minutes later, however, buoyed up by the floats that inflated automatically, and helicopters dropped a rescue crew of

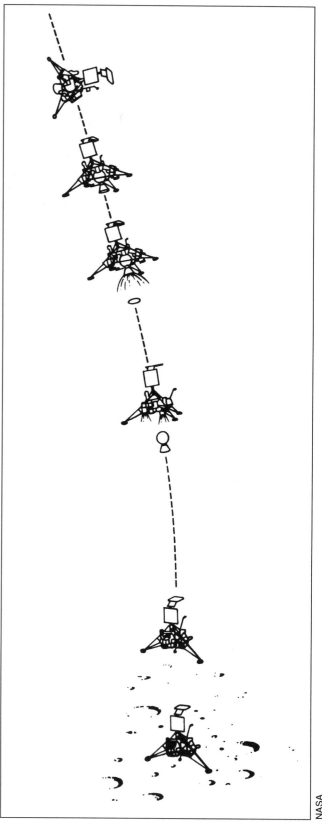

Surveyor probes made a soft landing on the moon to scout out possible Apollo landing sites

The Apollo Spacecraft

Country: U.S.

Crew: 3

Modules: 3

Command Module (CM): A cone-shaped module containing crew quarters, computer and manual control instruments
Height: 10.4 ft. (3.18 m)
Diameter: 12.8 ft. (3.9 m) at the base
Weight: 12,200 lb. (5,534 kg) at lift-off with astronauts; 11,700 lb. (5,307 kg) at splashdown

Service Module (SM): Cylindrical storage and propulsion unit
Height: 24.8 ft. (7.55 m) including engine nozzle
Diameter: 12.8 ft. (3.9 m)
Weight: 32,000 lb. (14,585 kg)

Lunar Module (LM): A two-part "Bug" or "Spider" vehicle for descent and ascent to and from the Moon
Height: 23.1 ft. (7.03 m) with legs fully extended
Diameter: 31 ft. (9.45 m) leg to leg
Weight: 32,500 lb. (14,752 kg) including propellants and astronauts

Conical in shape, the U.S. astronauts' passport to the Moon was designed to form the tip of the Saturn V rocket that carried it arching through Earth's atmosphere. At the nose of the spacecraft extended an attitude conttrol sensor, attitude control jets and an escape tower sitting atop the flattened cone shape of the Apollo Command Module. A heat shield protected the crew inside during launch. Beneath the Command Module sat the cylindrical Service Module with its rocket engine and high-gain antenna. Inside an adaptor container behind the Service Module, the Lunar Module was stored for later use at the Moon. An Instrument Unit connected the three-module spacecraft with the S-IVB third stage of the Saturn V launch booster.

Inside the nerve center of the spacecraft—the Command Module—each of the three crew members had about 69.6 cu ft. (1.97 cu m) of living space. Each astronaut had an adjustable couch for reclining, piloting or sitting upright. Five portholes to the outside, including one in the entrance hatch, made it possible to get a good view for docking, maneuvering and sightseeing. Space suits, tools and other equipment were stored beneath the couches. The center couch could fold out of the way so that two astronauts could stand in the center to use sextants, a telescope and so on. From the couches the crew could easily reach most of the 506 switches and watch the 71 lights and 40 indicators located above them.

While the main hatch (through which the astronauts entered feet first) was directly in front of the couches, a second hatch was located at the tip of the cone. The instrumentation for rendezvousing and docking with the Lunar Module was also located in this area of the Command Module and, once the LM was docked, the astronauts could enter it through this second hatch.

When it was time to return to Earth, the CM would go it alone. The pointed end contained the parachutes to slow the vehicle on reentry into the Earth's atmosphere. On reentry, the Apollo CM descended bottom downwards, using its flared base to shield its occupants from the heat and slow its descent.

After launch the escape tower, attitude control sensor and launch heat shield pulled away, and the S-IVB third stage of the booster refired from Earth orbit to set a new trajectory toward the Moon. Once on the way, the petals of the adaptor protecting the LM vehicle opened up. The CSM (Command and Service Module together) pulled away, reversed back to front, docked with the LM, and then pulled away from the third-stage rocket. The newly configured Apollo complex continued on to the Moon, the three parts of the spacecraft locked together.

The cylindrical Service Module, largest of the modules, formed the business end of the complex, housing an adjustable, restartable engine with a thrust of 20,503 lb. (9,300 kg). The engine could make trajectory corrections on the way to the Moon and, once the mission there was finished, it was the key to leaving lunar orbit and getting back to Earth. It also carried water, oxygen and fuel supplies for the complex. At the end of each mission, Apollo jettisoned the Service Module and it burned on reentry into the Earth's atmosphere.

The only part of the spacecraft to touch down on the Moon, the spider-like Lunar Module (see box) was actually made up of two parts—the Ascent Stage and a Descent Stage. Together they served as a lunar base for the two astronaut crews on the Moon's surface, housing living quarters, supplies, life-support systems, communications equipment and scientific equipment.

The first manned missions of the CSM were Apollo 7, launched into Earth orbit October 11, 1968, and Apollo 8, launched on a trip around the Moon on December 21. The first test of the LM with astronauts aboard was Apollo 9, launched March 3, 1969, in Earth orbit, while Apollo 10 astronauts headed for the Moon for the first time with the full complex on May 18.

frogmen and a dinghy. Soon the first Apollo astronauts were safely aboard the rescue carrier, with broad smiles on their faces. Apollo was finally on its way.

Apollo 8: Around the Moon!

Just two months later, buoyed with new confidence and spurred by two unmanned Soviet Zond missions to the Moon in October and November, NASA decided to use a Saturn V rocket to launch a crew for the first time. The Soviets had been sending probes to the Moon since the early 60s, but this was a new design. Were they also close to landing on the Moon? NASA's plan was a gamble—the most recent Saturn V test in April had showed signs of possible danger—vertical oscillations, or shaking, in stage 1 and partial failures in the engines of stages 2 and 3. An interim Earth-orbit test of the Lunar Module, originally planned to go next, wasn't ready, so the decision was made to bring in the crew from Apollo 9—astronauts Frank Borman, James Lovell and William Anders—and head out on a trip around the Moon.

As the final stage rocket powered up to exit Earth orbit, the craft hurtled through space at an escape velocity of 24,170 mph (38,898 km/h). Once on their way to the Moon, the Apollo 8 crew separated from the rocket, station-kept briefly for practice, and then, pared down to just Command and Service Modules, sped on their way.

With Apollo 8 already halfway to the Moon, Mission Control suddenly discovered tapes of data and crew comments revealing that Borman had been suffering an attack of flu symptoms—nausea, vomiting and diarrhea—during the flight. Could the situation become severely hazardous if all three astronauts came down with the symptoms? Should the spacecraft be brought back? When Borman maintained he'd recovered fully, they decided the mission would go on.

High anxiety invaded Mission Control in Houston, Texas, as the now-distant spacecraft slowed for arrival at the Moon, then prepared to streak around to the far side, where the Service Module's engine would kick on, placing Apollo 8 in Moon orbit. If the engine didn't work, the astronauts would either crash into the Moon or be sent careening back toward Earth. Yet, at this critical point in the mission, with the astronauts behind the Moon, no communication would be possible. "We'll see you on the other side," came Lovell's parting words across the 200,000 miles (321,860 km) of empty space. More than half an hour of silence followed. At last the anxious listeners heard Lovell's welcome voice again: "Go ahead, Houston, Apollo 8." The room went wild with cheers; they made it. It was Christmas Eve.

As Apollo circled the Moon for 20 hours, making a total 10 revolutions, the astronauts took films and photos of the far side, never before seen (except for photos taken by a Soviet unmanned Luna mission in 1959). On the near side as well they recorded craters, rilles and potential landing sites for missions to come. In an historic photograph Frank Borman captured a

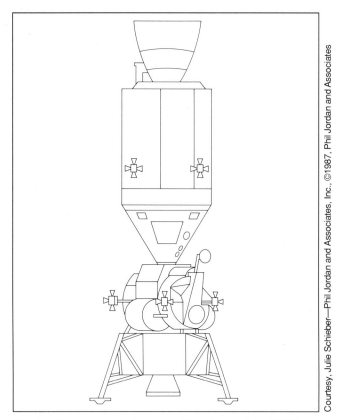

Courtesy, Julie Schieber—Phil Jordan and Associates, Inc., ©1987, Phil Jordan and Associates

The Apollo spacecraft: Command/Service module (CSM) and Lunar module (LM)

stunning view of Earth rising over the Moon, and the crew enraptured TV audiences with two broadcasts from the Moon.

The return trip went smoothly, brightened by two more TV broadcasts. As it returned to the Earth's atmosphere, Apollo 8 reentered at the incredible speed of 24,628 mph (39,635 km/h)—faster than any other manned spacecraft had ever done. Traveling at that speed, the capsule bounced like a ping-pong ball off the Earth's dense atmosphere before continuing safely downward on its descent path. For an agonizing five minutes the capsule was out of touch with ground control, but all went well—at the end of the six-day, three-hour mission, Apollo 8 splashed down right on time in the Pacific Ocean on December 27.

The first humans to ever travel to the Moon, Borman, Lovell and Anders had crossed some 233,014 miles (375,000 km) from the surface of the Earth into interplanetary space. They had orbited our only natural satellite at a distance of only 70 miles (112 km). They had seen various landing sites being considered for future missions and had found that they were, indeed, practical. They had shown that communications with ground control and support from Kennedy Space Center and Houston were adequate for such a distant mission. They had gone where no one had ever ventured before. Most important, they had shown that a crew could fly to the Moon, travel around it and return safely to Earth.

NASA

Apollo 8 lifts off, the crescent of the moon it's heading for shining in the background

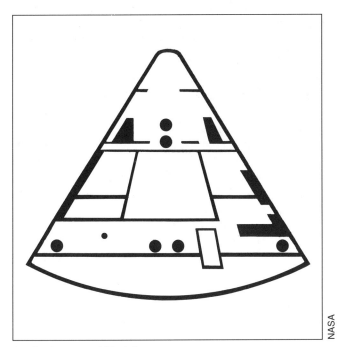

NASA

Apollo Command Module

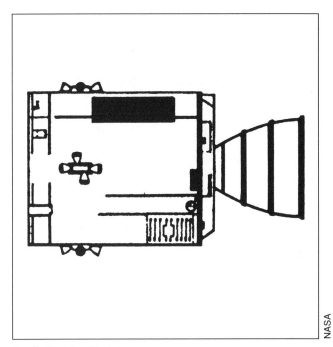

NASA

Apollo Service Module

NASA

Apollo 10 recovery, May 26, 1969, in the choppy waves of the South Pacific

Apollo 9: Trying Out the Lunar Module

For Apollo 9, the planned mission was more practical and less glamorous, but no less vital to the ultimate goal of putting a man on the Moon. Like the crews of the previous two missions, the Apollo 9 crew was plagued with minor illness—colds and sore throats—possibly because of excessive training demands, and the launch date had to be set back two days. Finally, on March 3, 1969, James McDivitt, David Scott and Russell Schweickart set off into Earth orbit to make the first manned space-borne tests of the full set of hardware required for a lunar landing.

After unlocking from the final rocket stage, the Apollo CSM, renamed "Gumdrop," completed its rear-to-front maneuver, rendezvoused, and docked with the LM that had been traveling tucked behind it. Schweickart and McDivitt transferred through the docking tunnel to the Lunar Module, nicknamed "Spider," undocked from Gumdrop, and took the strange, angular craft out for a spin. They put 100 miles (160 km) of distance between themselves and Scott aboard the CSM, followed by a successful rendezvous and redocking.

Suffering from the nausea and vomiting of space sickness, Rusty Schweickart trimmed a planned 2-hour EVA down to 67 minutes on the LM access platform, testing the Apollo lunar space suit and the strength of the LM ladder that would drop down to the Moon's surface. Meanwhile, Scott performed a stand-up EVA at the same time from the CM hatch for 62 minutes.

The flight lasted 10 days, one hour, one minute and splashed down in the Atlantic on March 13.

Apollo 10: Final Dress Rehearsal

Almost all the pieces were in place now, with only one more test to go. We knew we could fly around the Moon. We knew the Lunar Module worked well in Earth orbit. Before taking the final step, however, NASA wanted to know that the Lunar Module would function reliably in orbit around the Moon. Eugene Cernan, John Young and Thomas Stafford took Apollo 10 out for this final test jaunt, launching May 18, 1969.

The flight was in every way a dress rehearsal, completing all but the final landing step. In Moon orbit, Stafford and Cernan separated "Snoopy," the Apollo 10 LM, from "Charlie Brown," the CSM, and took it out for a test run. Circling the Moon four times and descending twice to within 50,000 feet (15,240 m) of the lunar surface, they sent back 19 color TV transmissions. At this height they were still within rescue range by pilot John Young aboard "Charlie Brown," who could have swooped down to pick them up in an emergency. Meanwhile Young completed a total of 32 revolutions around the Moon alone in the incredible vastness of space. Despite a violent jolt caused by an open switch when he jettisoned the lunar descent module (which in an actual landing would be left on the Moon), Cernan then boosted altitude on "Snoopy" to rejoin the CSM. He successfully redocked with "Charlie Brown," and the crew returned to Earth, splashing down in the Pacific on May 26. Their eight-day, three-minute dress rehearsal had been a resounding success.

At last, the long-awaited moment was at hand.

Milestones in Space: The Apollo Years, 1967-1972

1961   October 27: First test of the Saturn I rocket—a success

1964   May 28: A Saturn I rocket placed the first Apollo Command Module (CM) in orbit from Cape Kennedy

1967   January 27: Apollo 1, which was to be Apollo's first flight in Earth orbit, ended in tragedy when a fire breaks out during a ground testing at Cape Kennedy with the astronaut crew aboard. Edward White, Virgil Grissom and Roger Chaffee all died in the fire

November 9: The first launch with a Saturn V vehicle sends Apollo 4 into orbit for an unmanned test of both launcher and spacecraft. The test shows that the Saturn-Apollo combination could reach the Moon

1968   January 22: Apollo 5, launched atop a Saturn IB launcher in the first flight test of the propulsion systems of the Lunar Module ascent and descent stages

April 4: Apollo 6, launched by a Saturn V in another unmanned test, reveals problems with the launch vehicle, but the spacecraft performs well

October 11: Apollo 7, launched by a Saturn IB launcher in the first manned test of the Command Module, with Walter Schirra, Donn Eisele, and Walter Cunningham aboard. The flight lasted 260 hours, eight minutes, and descended on October 22

December 21: Apollo 8, the first manned Saturn V flight, takes astronauts Frank Borman, James Lovell, Jr. and William Anders into orbit around the Moon. They return after 10 lunar orbits for a December 27 splashdown

1969   March 3: Apollo 9 took James McDivitt, David Scott and Russell Schweickart into Earth orbit in the first manned test of all the hardware needed for a lunar landing. Schweickart performed an EVA from the LM while Scott extended head and shoulders from the CM, and McDivitt and Schweickart took the LM "Spider" out for the first manned flight, followed by a successful rendezvous and docking with the CM "Gumdrop." Recovery in the Atlantic completed the 10-day flight on March 13.

May 18: Apollo 10, with Eugene Cernan, John Young, and Thomas Stafford aboard, runs the last dress rehearsal for a Moon landing. Stafford and Cernan take the LM "Snoopy" for a test run down to within 10 miles (16 km) of the Moon's surface. Nineteen color TV transmissions are made, and the splashdown in the Pacific goes smoothly on May 26 after completion of the 192-hour, three minute mission

July 16: Apollo 11 launches with astronauts Neil Armstrong, Michael Collins and Edward Aldrin, Jr. aboard

July 20: Flying the Lunar Module "Eagle," Neil Armstrong and Ed Aldrin make the first manned landing on the Moon. While they spend 20 hours on the Moon's surface and take a two-hour moonwalk, Collins remains in the CM "Columbia." The three return for splashdown on July 24

November 14: Charles Conrad, Jr., Richard Gordon, Jr. and Alan Bean take Apollo 12 to the Moon for the second manned landing. On November 18, Conrad and Bean land on the Ocean of Storms near the unmanned Surveyor 3 landing site. They spend 7.5 hours walking on the Moon's surface. The mission ends with splashdown in the Pacific on November 24

1970   April 11: Apollo 13 launches for a planned third Moon landing near the crater Fra Mauro. But an explosion aboard the CM "Odyssey" on April 13

causes NASA to scrap the plan. Astronauts James Lovell, Jr., John Swigert and Fred Haise, Jr. climb into the LM "Aquarius" as they loop around the Moon and use it as a lifeboat to return to Earth, with a safe splashdown on April 17 after their harrowing six-day trip

1971   January 31: Apollo 14, the third manned lunar landing, puts astronauts Alan Shepard and Edgar Mitchell on the Moon in the lunar module "Antares" on February 5 while Stuart Roosa pilots the command module. Shepard and Mitchell perform moonwalks at Fra Mauro for a total of nine hours and bring back 98 pounds of lunar material. Total flight time for the mission: 216 hours, 42 minutes, with splashdown in the Pacific Ocean on February 9

July 26: Apollo 15 launches for the fourth lunar landing—the first to carry the Lunar Roving Vehicle. Astronauts: David R. Scott, Alfred M. Worden, James B. Irwin. Scott and Irwin spend three days on the Moon near Hadley Rille. Worden performs an in-flight EVA for 38 minutes, 12 seconds. They splash down August 7, bringing back 173 pounds of lunar material

1972   April 16: Apollo 16 takes astronauts John W. Young, Thomas K. Mattingly II, and Charles M. Duke, Jr. to the Moon. The CM "Casper" develops engine troubles, delaying lunar landing, but Young and Duke spend three days with the lunar rover near the crater Descartes on the lunar surface. Successful splashdown in the Pacific Ocean on April 27 with 213 pounds of "Moon rocks"

December 7: Apollo 17, the sixth and last lunar landing, puts Eugene Cernan and Harrison Schmitt on the Moon for a total of 22 hours, four minutes of EVAs each. Ronald Evans piloted the CM. The mission brought back 243 pounds of lunar samples, with splashdown on December 19

11

SOYUZ: LONG-TERM PASSPORT TO SPACE

The sight of the spaceships flying so freely in space made an enormous impression on me. It was a wonderful sight . . .
— Yevgeny Khrunov, after the docking of Soyuz 5 with Soyuz 4

It took 18 long months for the Soviet Soyuz program to recover from the Soyuz 1 disaster while investigations and unmanned testing progressed. In addition to Komarov's death, the Soviet space program was still affected by the untimely death of chief designer Sergei Korolev in early 1966. Soyuz would be part of a master plan though—it was to be the major bus system to Soviet space stations of the future.

Meanwhile, 1968 saw the first of a series of four unmanned capsules sent by the Soviets around the Moon. Named Zond probes, these may in fact have been unmanned Soyuz spacecraft preparing for a Soviet manned Moon mission. That mission never materialized, but by late October 1968, just two weeks after the first manned Apollo flight in the U.S. (see Chapter 10), the Soviets were ready for a second one-man test flight of the Soyuz craft.

Soyuz 2 and 3

This time the Soviets would try rendezvousing with a dummy (empty) Soyuz spacecraft—a first step toward the future for which Soyuz was designed (its name means "union"). On October 25, Soyuz 2 was launched empty, followed the next day by Georgy Beregovoy aboard Soyuz 3.

Under automatic control, Soyuz 3 approached its target to within less than 200 yards (180 m). Then, after the spacecraft backed away to a distance of 350 miles (565 km), Beregovoy brought it back in under manual control to rendezvous again with Soyuz 2. However, although docking was apparently planned for the mission, none took place.

Soyuz 2 reentered the atmosphere under automatic control on October 28, running a successful test on the parachute system. Meanwhile, Beregovoy stayed in orbit for a total of four days, making numerous TV reports to Earth and completing weather studies and photography. His return to Earth on October 30 at the end of his 64-orbit mission went smoothly; he descended right on target and within view of the search party.

A collective sigh of relief must have been breathed throughout the Soviet space program. With Beregovoy back safe and sound, the Soyuz 2-3 mission had showed that the Soviets would recover from the loss of Korolev, the throes of the Soyuz 1 disaster and the death of cosmonaut Yuri Gagarin in a training plane accident in March 1968. Like the U.S., the Soviets were back in "manned" space once again.

The Soyuz Spacecraft

Country: USSR

Crew: Three (at first), later two

Modules: Three: a conical living/working quarters, a cylindrical propulsion/instrumentation module, oval descent module

Diameter: Between 7.5 and 9.7 ft. (2.29 and 2.97 m)

Total Length: 34 ft. (10.36 m)

Total Weight: 13,228 lb. (6,000 kg)

The Soyuz spacecraft, first flown by Vladimir Komarov on the ill-fated Soyuz 1 mission, has, in various configurations, formed the basic transportation system for cosmonauts to and from space since 1968. Its name means "union," and its chief purpose is to ferry crews to and from a space station for extended work. There the Soyuz docks and, in the early models, could stay only for up to 30 days.

However, the Soviets early devised a scheme of sending visiting crews to bring a fresh Soyuz and return home in the flagging Soyuz after a short visit.

On the return trip to Earth, the cosmonauts enter the hermetically sealed environment of the Soyuz reentry capsule. The atmosphere is a mixture of oxygen and nitrogen at sea level pressure. The outside of the oval-shaped pod is heavily shielded against heat, and the descent is braked both by a parachute and by retrorockets that fire shortly before the capsule reaches the ground. The capsule has three windows, and the cosmonauts wear space suits during descent.

The Orbital Module has enough room inside for crew members to stand up and includes an area for working and sleeping, with a "sideboard" area for preparing food and doing scientific experiments. When crew members perform EVAs the craft doubles as an airlock; when the hatch to the reentry module is sealed, the Orbital Module can be depressurized and the cosmonauts can exit into space.

Either an adaptor cone or a docking probe in the nose of the Orbital Module enables it to dock with a Salyut space station, and the crew enters the space station through the hatch in the nose.

The Instrumentation Module is an inaccessible service area where two wing-like solar panels are attached and which contains the computer and the various life-support propulsion and control systems necessary to run the craft.

While the Soyuz failed frequently in the early years, continual upgrading and improvement since then have made it a reliable, steady way to get "from here to there."

Soyuz 4 and 5

Eleven weeks later, with the launches of Soyuz 4 and 5, the Soyuz program appeared to have put its problems behind it. The dual-spacecraft mission included the first docking of two manned spacecraft and the first transfer of humans from spacecraft to spacecraft.

Soyuz 4, with Vladimir Shatalov flying alone with two empty seats, was the first to enter orbit, lifting off from the Tyuratam launch site on January 14. Soyuz 5 followed the next day, piloted by Boris Volynov, with Yevgeny Khrunov (research engineer) and Alexei Yeliseyev (flight engineer) as passengers. Under automatic control the two vehicles rendez-voused on January 16 to within 110 yards (100 m), when Shatalov took over manual control and brought Soyuz 4 in to dock successfully with Soyuz 5. Yeliseyev and Khrunov then put on space suits, ex-ited through the Soyuz 5 side hatch and used hand-rails to travel to Soyuz 4 in a 37-minute space walk. The two passengers climbed aboard Soyuz 4 while the two spacecraft remained linked nose to nose for a total of five hours. Yeliseyev and Khrunov then returned to Earth aboard Soyuz 4 with Shatalov on January 17, with Volynov returning by himself the next day.

The mission was an unqualified success—the Soviet's first in four years—but it may have seemed less significant than the U.S. Apollo 8 mission the previous month that had sent three men into orbit around the Moon and back. While the Soyuz 4-5 mission in a sense demonstrated the feasibility of space rescue and space assembly (for which docking and transfer between spacecraft would be necessary), the Soviets had docked spacecraft before (though never both manned) and a spacecraft-to-spacecraft space walk had been done in 1966 by U.S. Gemini astronauts working on the Agena satellite. Transfer

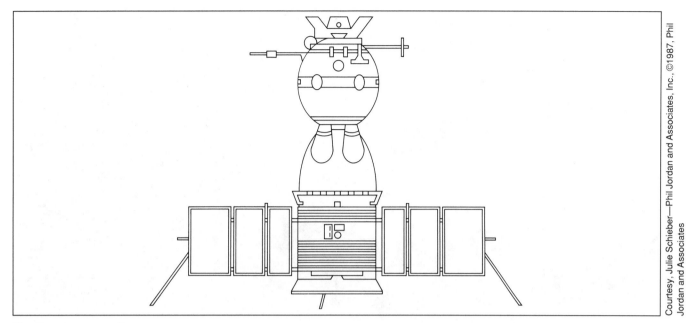

The Soyuz spacecraft

through a docking tunnel (developed by the Americans for the Apollo program) would also be adopted by the Soviets for future missions. In reality, in 1969 the Soyuz program was marking time.

Soyuz 6, 7 and 8

The Soviets would not launch another manned mission until the following fall, while the U.S. continued its successful Apollo program to the Moon. Claiming that the "Moon Race" was a figment of the American imagination and that they had never intended to go to the Moon, the Soviets began to move in another direction, which they would continue throughout the 1980s: long-duration space missions.

In late 1969, however, they were still a long way from launching their new Salyut space station. In the meantime, for international political reasons, they needed a manned space "event." On October 11, 12 and 13, therefore, they launched the first "space squadron," consisting of three spacecraft orbiting at one time.

Soyuz 6 went first, with Georgy Shonin in command and Valery Kubasov as flight engineer. Soyuz 7 followed the next day, commanded by Anatoly Filipchenko and carrying Vladislav Volkov (flight engineer) and Viktor Gorbatko (research engineer). The final ship of the "space squadron" was manned by Vladimir Shatalov (commander) and Alexei Yeliseyev, who had flown in the Soyuz 4-5 flights only 10 months earlier.

The plan called for Soyuz 8 to dock with Soyuz 7. They hovered within 500 yards (488 m) of each other on October 15, remaining in rendezvous for 24 hours while Soyuz 6 looked on, but backed off without docking.

Aboard Soyuz 6, Shonin and Kubasov closed themselves off in their reentry module and depressurized the orbiting workshop, so they could perform a remote-control welding experiment in the vacuum and weightlessness of space—the first such experiment ever performed. They returned to Earth on October 16, followed by Soyuz 7 on October 17 and Soyuz 8 on October 18—with a total mission time of four days and just under 23 hours in space for each crew.

Soyuz 9

The following year saw the Soviets' first long-duration spaceflight with Andrian Nikolayev and Vitaly Sevastyanov's 18-day mission aboard Soyuz 9. Launched June 1, 1970, their mission broke the 14-day record previously set by the U.S. Gemini 7 crew in 1965. In space, Sevastyanov and Nikolayev completed extensive studies of ocean currents and surface temperatures, primarily for use by the Soviet fishing industry.

Nikolayev, a veteran of the Vostok 3 mission eight years before, had married Valentina Tereshkova, who had flown in Vostok 6. Now, from Flight Control their daughter Elena celebrated her sixth birthday with her

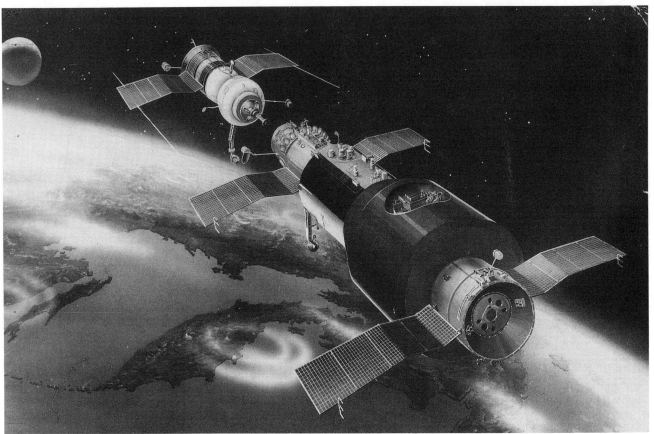

An artist's conception shows Soyuz 11 approaching to dock with Salyut 1

Sovfoto

father via the ground-to-Soyuz communications system.

For the first time, with the Soyuz 9 return descent on June 19, the Soviets recorded the return of one of their spacecraft on TV. All went well, but when the exhausted cosmonauts landed, they had to be carried from their spacecraft. They later complained of difficulty readjusting to Earth gravity, commenting for several days afterward that they felt like they were trying to move about inside a centrifuge.

Soyuz 10 and 11

With the launch of the Salyut 1 space station on April 19, 1971, it seemed the Soviet program was now truly up and running with a new, high-potential thrust: long-duration spaceflight and a permanent presence in space.

Soyuz 10, launched four days after Salyut, docked successfully with the space station on April 24, with Vladimir Shatalov, Alexei Yeliseyev and Nikolai Rukavishnikov aboard. The cosmonauts could not get into the space station, however. Disappointed, they

had to scrap their plans to spend 30 days in their brand-new orbiting home and returned to Earth the next day.

The Soyuz 11 mission, launched June 6 with Georgy Dobrovolsky, Vladislov Volkov and Viktor Patsayev aboard, went better, at first. The three succeeded in docking with Salyut and then entered and spent 23 days on the station, but on their return trip, a valve malfunction in their Soyuz descent module caused the cabin to depressurize. The three cosmonauts were found dead inside the capsule when it landed on June 30, 1971.

The loss of the Soyuz crew was an enormous human tragedy that shook the Soviet people, who displayed a public grief similar to that Americans felt at President Kennedy's assassination in 1963 or the *"Challenger"* shuttle accident in 1986. In addition, it was a severe blow to the Soviet program, which would not venture another Soyuz launch until the spacecraft was redesigned and thoroughly tested. Not until September 1973, more than two years later, would the crippled Soyuz-Salyut program once more get off the ground.

The crew of the Soyuz 11—Viktor Patsayev (l), Georgy Dobrovolsky and Vladislov Volkov—all 3 died on the return trip after a 23-day stay aboard the Salyut 1 space station

Sovfoto

Milestones in Space: Soyuz Missions 1967-1971

1967   Soyuz 1   April 23   Komarov

First manned test flight of the Soyuz spacecraft, ending in tragedy on reentry on April 24, resulting in the death of veteran cosmonaut Vladimir Komarov

1968   Soyuz 2   October 25
**   Soyuz 3   October 26   Beregovoy**

Soyuz 3, piloted by Georgy Beregovoy, rendezvoused successfully with the unmanned Soyuz 2 spacecraft but did not dock. Soyuz 2 returned to Earth October 28, while Beregovoy and Soyuz 3 continued a 4-day mission, totaling 64 orbits, before successful return on October 30

1969   Soyuz 4   January 14   Shatalov
**   Soyuz 5   January 15   Volynov,**
**   Khrunov, Yeliseyev**

Piloted by Vladimir Shatalov, Soyuz 4 rendezvoused with Soyuz 5 in the first manned docking and the first EVA transfer from one manned vehicle to another. Soyuz 5 carried three cosmonauts (Boris Volynov, commander; Yevgeny Khrunov, research engineer; and Alexei Yeliseyev, flight engineer) into orbit. After successful docking, the two Soyuz 5 passengers transferred to return in Soyuz 4 on January 17, leaving Volynov to return to Earth alone on the 18th

Soyuz 6   October 11   Shonin, Kubasov
Soyuz 7   October 12   Filipchenko,
Gorbatko, Volkov
Soyuz 8   October 13   Shatalov,
Yeliseyev

Three manned Soyuz spacecraft launched one after the other, each orbiting for a total of five days. Soyuz 7 and 8 rendezvoused to within about 500 yards (488 m), maintaining the distance for about 24 hours, with Soyuz 6 watching from nearby. The Soyuz 6 crew tried out experimental welding equipment by remote control

**1970   Soyuz 9   June 1   Nikolayev, Sevas-
tyanov**

Long-duration record established in an 18-day mission by two-man crew: Andrian Nikolayev, commander, and Vitaly Sevastyanov, flight engineer. Returned on June 19

**1971   Soyuz 10   April 23   Shatalov,
Yeliseyev, Rukavishnikov**

Launched four days after the new Salyut space station, the Soyuz 10 mission docked successfully with the station but the crew was unable to enter and had to cancel a planned 30-day stay. Soyuz 10 returned to Earth April 25

**Soyuz 11 June 6   Dobrovolsky, Volkov,
Patsayev**

Soyuz 11 made a second attempt to be the first space-station mission and succeeded in docking, entering and completing a 23-day stay aboard Salyut. The mission ended in tragedy, however, when a valve malfunction depressurized the cabin on reentry on June 30, killing the entire crew

NASA

The X-15 experimental aircraft riding below the wing of a B-52

NASA

Neil Armstrong and the X-15

Yuri Gagarin inside Vostok.

John Glenn during first US orbital flight

Mercury-Redstone 3 lifts off with Alan Shepard aboard

Vostok launch

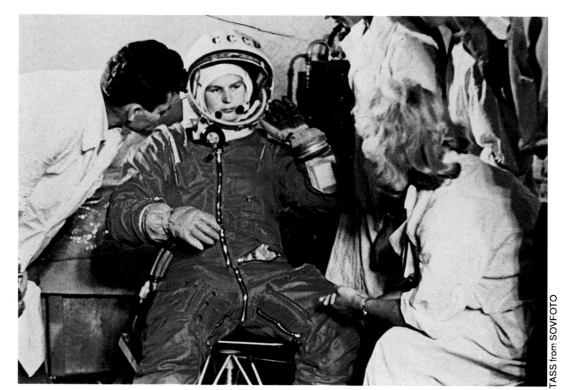

Valentina Tereshkova, the first woman in space.

Ed White's EVA during the Gemini 4 mission

NASA

Apollo 8 view of the Moon on first manned flight around the Moon

NASA

Gemini 7 as seen from Gemini 6

NASA

Earthrise above the Moon as seen from Apollo 8

NASA

James Irwin during Apollo 15 EVA

Apollo 11 Lunar Module pilot Buzz Aldrin during the first mission to the surface of the Moon. (Note Neil Armstrong's reflection in Aldrin's face mask.)

NASA

Apollo 17 lift-off

Antennas like this one at Goldstone in the California Mojave Desert helped keep in touch with Apollo spacecraft during missions

Astronauts Tom Stafford and John Young await recovery in the Pacific Ocean after Apollo 10 mission. (Gene Cernan is already on board the helicopter.)

PART 3

TAKING THE GIANT STEP
TO THE MOON

12

"THE EAGLE HAS LANDED": APOLLO 11

This has been far more than three men on a mission to the Moon; more still than the efforts of a government and industry team; more, even, than the efforts of one nation. We feel this stands as a symbol of the insatiable curiosity of all mankind to explore the unknown.
—Buzz Aldrin in a broadcast from Apollo 11

Less than two months after Cernan, Young and Stafford had returned from the Moon on their Apollo 10 dry run, the day for Apollo 11 finally dawned. It may have looked like any other mid-July day in Florida, but this was the day for which more than 300,000 Americans had worked over a period of 10 years, through the development of the Saturn rocket, Project Mercury, Project Gemini and seven earlier Apollo flights, both manned and unmanned.

The crew, made up entirely of veterans of the Gemini program, included Neil Armstrong as commander. An engineer and test pilot, he once flew the X-15 above 200,000 feet and at more than 4,000 mph and flew in space aboard Gemini 8. Air Force Colonel Edwin E. "Buzz" Aldrin had previously piloted Gemini 12. Now he was scheduled to pilot the Lunar Module (LM) "Eagle" in its descent to the Moon's surface and on its journey back to rejoin the Command/Service Module (CSM) "Columbia." A graduate of West Point (third in his class), he had also earned a Ph.D. in astronautics at MIT. Meanwhile, in lunar orbit, Michael Collins would pilot the "Columbia" alone for 24 hours while Armstrong and Aldrin descended on their great adventure to the surface. Also a West

Pointer, he was a lieutenant colonel in the Air Force and had flown aboard Gemini 10.

Getting There

Some one billion people were estimated to be watching all over the world at 9:32 A.M. Eastern Daylight Time (Kennedy Space Center—the time of the launch is set at KSC, then Mission Control in Houston takes over) when the big rocket began to belch fire and dense smoke as it thundered skyward that day, July 16. Inside, the lift-off's hiccupping and jerking made for a rough ride, but the craft finally settled down after a few seconds. Apollo 11 was in Earth orbit within 12 minutes of lift-off.

Just two hours and 44 minutes from launch, the rocket entered its third stage and the Apollo crew moved out of Earth orbit to head for the Moon. It was now time for the slow separation from the third stage and the 180-degree about-face required to dock with the LM Eagle and pull it away from its safe traveling place inside the rocket's adaptor. All went smoothly as the rocket went its separate way, and Eagle and Columbia sped locked together toward the Moon.

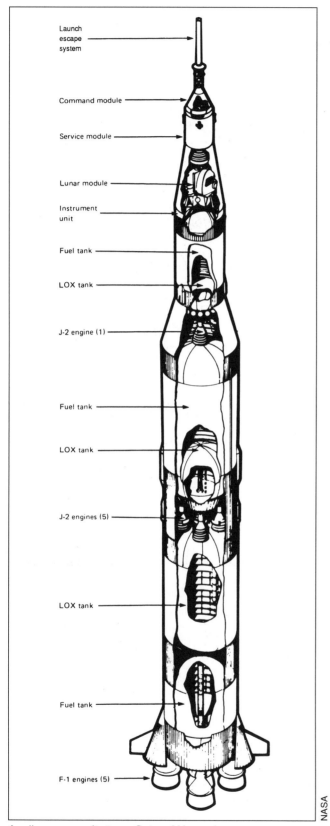

Launch
escape
system

Command module

Service module

Lunar module

Instrument
unit

Fuel tank

LOX tank

J-2 engine (1)

Fuel tank

LOX tank

J-2 engines (5)

LOX tank

Fuel tank

F-1 engines (5)

NASA

Apollo spacecraft atop a Saturn V Launcher

As the crew neared their goal at the end of the long cruise, they exclaimed on the extraordinary view of the Moon through their port. The spectacular sight of the giant disc filling three-quarters of the hatch window was, as Armstrong put it, "a view worth the price of the trip."

After 75 hours and 41 minutes of flight, Apollo 11 arrived at the Moon and disappeared, like Apollo 8 and 10, "around the corner" out of sight, where the Columbia engines placed them into orbit at 70 miles (113 km), and preparations began for the all-important landing.

The Eagle Has Landed

On July 20, Armstrong and Aldrin entered the Eagle through the docking hatch while Collins remained in control of the Columbia. Aldrin backed the Eagle away and shortly after 3:00 P.M. (Central Daylight Time—Houston time, where Mission Control was watching every move), he brought the LM down to within 50,000 feet of the lunar surface and burned the descent rocket to slow down for a soft landing.

At this stage the mission was almost aborted when problems with an overloaded computer raised questions about its accuracy in calculating altitude and rate of descent for the Eagle. At 6,562 feet (2,000 m) Mission Control carefully deliberated the safety of the mission. Would the computer clear itself? Finally the quiet order came, "Go, Flight."

In the last 492 feet (150 m), however, as they neared the surface, Armstrong decided to finish the approach under manual control to avoid a group of hazardous boulders in the landing area on the Sea of Tranquility.

As the Eagle settled gently down on the broad, dry, flat plain of the Sea of Tranquility, probes extending out from the Eagle's legs triggered a contact light to advise the pilot. Aldrin and Armstrong could feel the legs settle firmly moments later. In close radio contact with Houston Mission Control, Aldrin kept a steady patter of technical reports going, until, at last, safely arrived, the engine shut down, Armstrong announced the news over the intercom, "Houston, Tranquility Base here. The Eagle has landed." Only 2 percent of the descent fuel remained.

"One small step"

The two astronauts decided not to rest for four hours as planned but to begin preparations right away for their moon walk. Wearing their white pressurized suits and helmets, they depressurized the cramped interior of the LM and, finally, after much longer

FLIGHT PROFILE

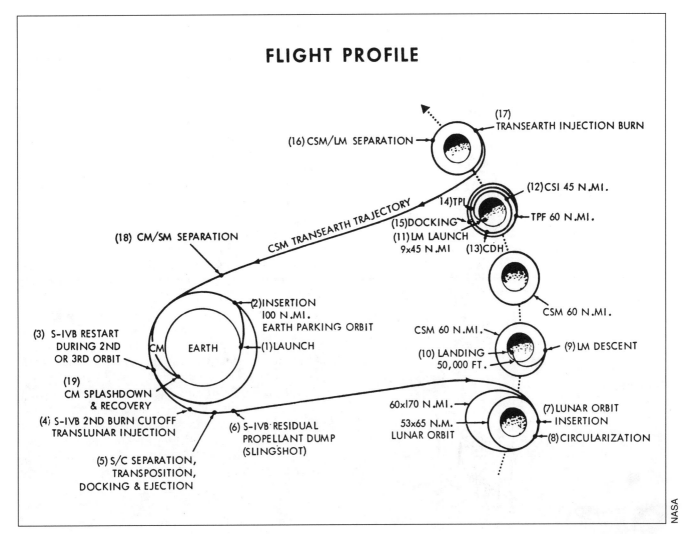

A typical Apollo lunar landing mission

The Lunar Module

Country: U.S.

Crew: 2

Modules: 2, a descent stage and an ascent stage

Height: 23.1 ft. (7.03 m) with legs fully extended

Diameter: 31 ft. (9.45 m) leg to leg

Weight: 32,500 lb. (14,742 kg) including propellants and astronauts

Because the Lunar Module (LM) would never have to travel through the drag of Earth's atmosphere, its designers gave more thought to issues of weight (the lighter the module the less fuel would be spent in descent and ascent) than to aerodynamics. Consequently, it had an odd, angular, bug-like shape, with cantilevered landing legs. A 10-foot ladder extended down one leg from a hatch in the upper part of the module.

The LM left Earth hidden inside an adaptor fairing, a structure that reduces air resistance, on the third stage of the Saturn V rocket. After the trajectory to the Moon was set, the Apollo crews separated from the third stage and swung around to pluck the LM out of its hiding place. From there the LM traveled to the Moon docked to the Apollo Command/Service Module (CSM), and the astronauts entered it from the CM through a docking tunnel.

The lower portion of the module was the descent stage and carried an engine that could be throttled up to 10,000 pounds (4,535 kg) of thrust to enable a soft landing on the Moon's surface. When docked to the CSM it traveled engine outward and doubled as an emergency vehicle in the event the main Service Module engine failed. (Because the LM wasn't ready yet, though, Apollo 8 had gone to the Moon without this added insurance, making that trip doubly risky.)

From the surface of the Moon, the descent stage functioned as a launching platform for the ascent stage when the astronauts were ready to leave. The descent stage also carried the Lunar Roving Vehicle for the later "J-Series" missions.

The ascent stage provided a sort of mini-moon base, with a pressurized cabin and life-support systems. The ascent stage also had its own rocket engine, navigation and guidance systems, a computer and a radar altimeter.

To go out on an EVA, the astronauts pressurized their space suits, depressurized their cabin and exited through the EVA hatch to a platform, or porch, outside, then climbed down the ladder, jumping the last distance to the ground.

When it was time to leave the Moon, the astronauts traveled aboard the ascent stage, which became a separate spacecraft that could be piloted and could rendezvous and dock with the CSM. The descent stage was left behind in the lunar dust.

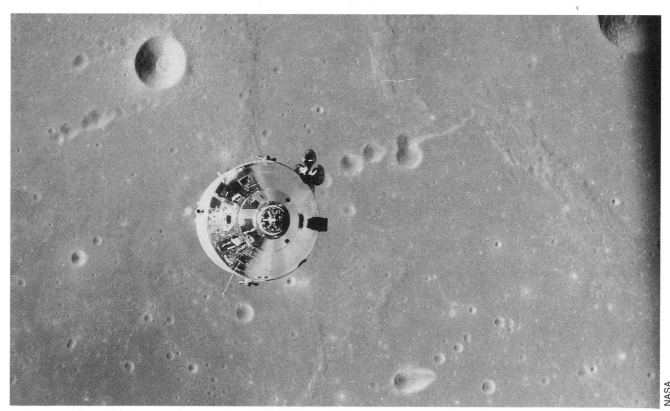

NASA

Apollo 11 CSM seen from the Lunar Module as they orbit above the Moon's surface

preparations than anticipated, opened the hatch onto a new world.

Millions of people tuned in their TVs as Armstrong backed out of the hatch, carefully ventured down the Eagle's 10-foot (3-m) ladder and, still hanging onto the ladder, extended one foot beyond the last rung. It was 9:56 P.M., Houston time, seven hours after touchdown, on Sunday, July 20, 1969, when Neil Armstrong made that first historic step to the surface of the Moon, as he announced to the world, "That's one small step for a man, one giant leap for mankind." TV viewers watched as he took a preliminary sample

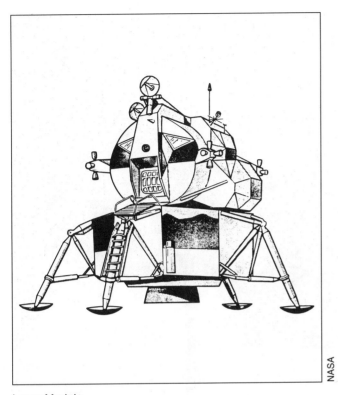

Lunar Module

of lunar soil, just in case a hasty retreat prevented later opportunities, and began elatedly describing the strange world around him.

Contrary to some expectations, his feet did not sink into deep, powdery dust—in fact the dust was barely an eighth of an inch thick at the landing site, he reported. He found the backpack life-support system and pressurized Apollo space suit easy to maneuver in, given the Moon's gravity equal to one-sixth of Earth's. Joined shortly by Aldrin, whose first words were an admiring "Beautiful view," the two began a two-and-a-half hour tour of a small patch of lunar soil near the Sea of Tranquility, never roaming farther than 197 feet (60 m) from the safety of the life-support system of the Eagle, which served as their "moon base" during their stay. They bounded about in the more weightless environment, strongly resembling kangaroos with fishbowl heads as they moved in long, bouncy strides. They set out experiments and gathered up 44 pounds (19.9 kg) of typical lunar material found in that area, including samples taken from as deep as 7 inches (18 cm). The average age of the samples they brought back was some four billion years.

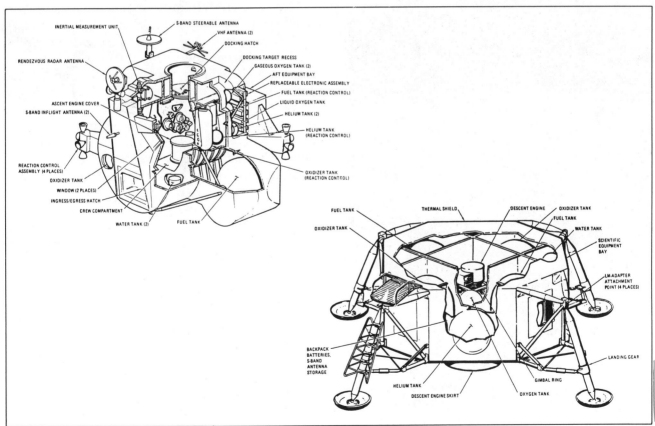

Ascent stage of Apollo Lunar Module

Descent stage of Apollo Lunar Module

NASA

Buzz Aldrin steps from the Eagle onto the Moon

The Eagle's footpad, surrounded by Armstrong and Aldrin's footprints on the Moon, July 20, 1969

Armstrong and Aldrin left behind a 169.8-pound (77-kg) package of scientific and experimental instruments as well as a silicon disc etched with messages of goodwill from leaders of 73 nations on Earth; medals given them by the families of cosmonauts Yuri Gagarin and Vladimir Komarov; an Apollo 1 flight patch in memory of astronauts Gus Grissom, Roger Chaffee, and Ed White; a 10-cent U.S. postage stamp commemorating the landing of the first man on the moon; and an American flag held taut by an aluminum frame in the breezeless environment.

Collins, meanwhile, orbiting alone in the Columbia, watched from above as the colors of the Moon shifted from gray to brown and back to gray in the changing light from the Sun. One day into the Apollo trip, the USSR had launched their Luna 15 probe to the Moon, which Mission Control initially worried would confuse communications with Apollo 11. The Soviets, however, assured there would be no problem, and, in fact, although Collins saw the probe orbiting below him as he circled the Moon in his long and lonely watch, no difficulty arose.

The first human visit on the surface of the Moon lasted 21 hours 36 minutes. At 12:55 P.M. on July 21, Aldrin and Armstrong lifted off in the Eagle's ascent module, leaving behind the descent stage, which bore a plaque commemorating their visit. At 70 miles (113 km) they joined Collins and the Columbia and,

Aldrin with the flag he and Armstrong erected on the Moon

wrenching themselves from the Moon's orbit, they thrusted away from its pull and headed for home.

Return to Earth

The Apollo 11 crew splashed down on July 24, at 12:51 P.M. EDT, their historic mission of eight days, three hours, 18 minutes complete. They now faced a three-week quarantine, since no one knew for certain whether they might be carrying microorganisms from the alien world from which they had just returned.

The lunar material they brought back, along with that collected in later missions, became the basis for close scientific scrutiny in an effort to crack the mysteries of the origin of the Moon, the Earth, the solar system and the universe itself.

Apollo 11 had been an enormous success. It had added invaluable information to our understanding of our closest neighbor in the solar system. Armstrong and Aldrin had seen it for themselves. They'd performed numerous experiments and left others behind. They'd photographed the terrain and taken samples of lunar soil. And they'd found out what it was like to walk on the Moon.

Men who followed would have the opportunity to find out even more about the Moon, but Neil Armstrong and Buzz Aldrin were the pioneers who led the way.

13

EXPLORING THE MOON: APOLLO 12-17

It makes me proud to be part of a country that can send a man 250,000 miles away from home, and even prouder to be part of a country that can bring him back.

—Ken Mattingly, Apollo 16

Apollo 11 was by no means the end of the Apollo story. Six more missions were completed—all but one of them landing on the Moon—and each one built on those that had preceded it. Before Apollo was finished, 12 human beings had walked on the Moon and left their footprints on the dusty surface, where, in the airless quiet, they doubtless will remain for eons to come—or until the next mission arrives.

Apollo 12: Moon Walks in November

By late fall 1969, the Apollo program was ready for its next trip to the Moon. With Charles "Pete" Conrad, Richard Gordon and Alan Bean aboard, Apollo 12 was launched on November 14 and its LM, "Intrepid," made its touchdown five days later on the Ocean of Storms, about 950 miles (1,500 km) from the Apollo 11 site. The crew made a highly successful precision landing less than 100 feet (30 m) from the target, and just 200 yards (185 m) from the unmanned Surveyor 3 probe that had landed there two and one-half years before. Bean and Conrad spent more than 30 hours on the surface, including two trips out from their base Intrepid, for a total EVA time between them of 15 hours, 32 minutes. Now that it was known that the Moon wasn't made of a fragile crust that might cave

in on a bottomless cavern at any misstep, Bean and Conrad roamed a little farther from the safety of the Intrepid.

While they were there, the Apollo team investigated the nearby Surveyor 3 spacecraft, retrieved parts of it and took photos of other possible exploration sites. The mission lasted 244 hours, 36 minutes, brought back 75 pounds of lunar material, and concluded with a successful splashdown on November 24.

Apollo 13: Unlucky Number?

While there's no such thing as an unlucky number, Apollo 13 astronauts James Lovell, Fred Haise and John Swigert must have wondered. Only 56 hours into their mission, launched April 11, 1970, Lovell's voice came across to Mission Control with the bad news: "Houston, we've had a problem here." At a distance of 205,000 miles (329,915 km) from Earth, an explosion in the Service Module had created a critical emergency situation, resulting in loss of all oxygen and electric power in the CSM. The rest of the mission, intended to land on the Moon, was immediately abandoned. All three astronauts crowded into the LM "Aquarius," where they lived for four days on supplies intended to maintain just two men for two days

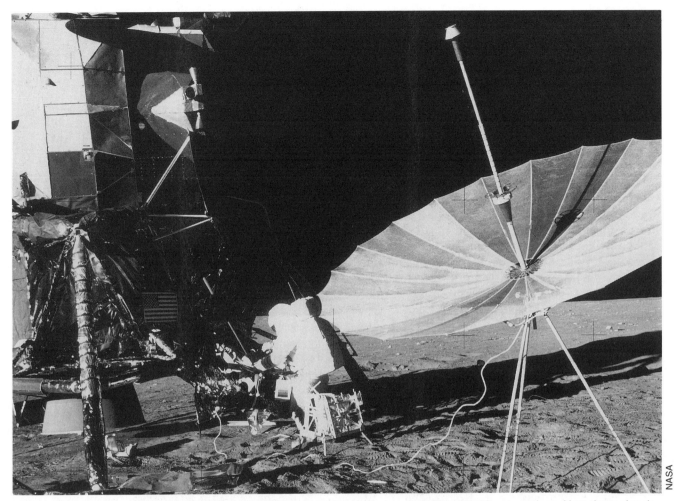

NASA

Apollo 12 Commander Charles Conrad works near the Lunar Module during an EVA on the Moon's surface. Note the tool rack by Conrad and the S-band antenna already erected on the right.

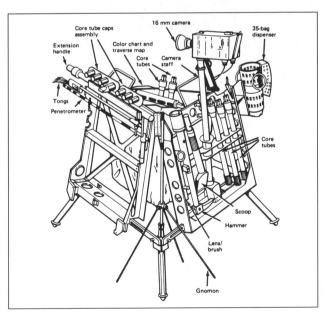

NASA

Tool rack used on lunar EVAs

on the lunar surface. They looped around the Moon and returned to Earth successfully on a free-return trajectory (a "free ride" from Earth's gravity), where they jettisoned the severely damaged SM about five hours before reentry and, back in the CM again, jettisoned their Aquarius LM lifeboat about three hours away from reentry. The whole world watched breathlessly, including tens of thousands of technicians and ground crew who had helped handle the emergency. Apollo 13 splashed down safely six days after lift-off on April 17. It had been much too close a call. Naturally the men were sorry they'd missed their chance to roam about on the Moon but they were enormously glad to be home.

Apollo 14: "Antares" at Fra Mauro

The next venture wasn't ready to go until the following year. Launched January 31, Apollo 14 carried astronauts Alan Shepard (who had pioneered in the first manned Mercury flight), Stuart Roosa and Edgar Mitchell. Shepard, the only one of the original Mercury Seven to go to the Moon, and Roosa took the LM "Antares" down to the Moon's surface on February 5. They used a two-wheel trolley to haul samples near the crater Fra Mauro, and Shepard became the first person ever to golf on the Moon. The two spent nine hours in EVA during two moon walks. They returned to the CSM "Kitty Hawk," where Mitchell had been orbiting and headed for home to splash down in the Pacific Ocean on February 9. Their total flight time was nine days, 42 minutes, and they had 98 pounds of lunar material aboard. Because no evidence of any life on the Moon had been found in all this time, Mitchell, Shepard and Roosa were the last to undergo the 21-day quarantine upon return that had been established with Apollo 11.

Apollo 15: "Roving" on the Lunar Surface

With Apollo 15, a new era of manned Moon exploration began. Called the first of the Apollo "J" series of

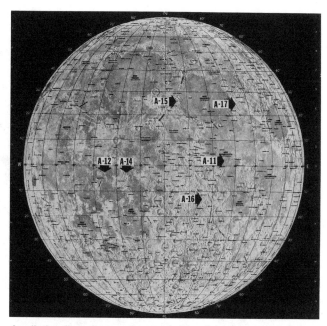

Apollo landing sites on the near side of the Moon: Apollo 11, Sea of Tranquility; Apollo 12, Ocean of storms; Apollo 14, Fra Mauro; Apollo 15, Hadley Apennines; Apollo 16, Descartes; and Apollo 17, Taurus Littrow

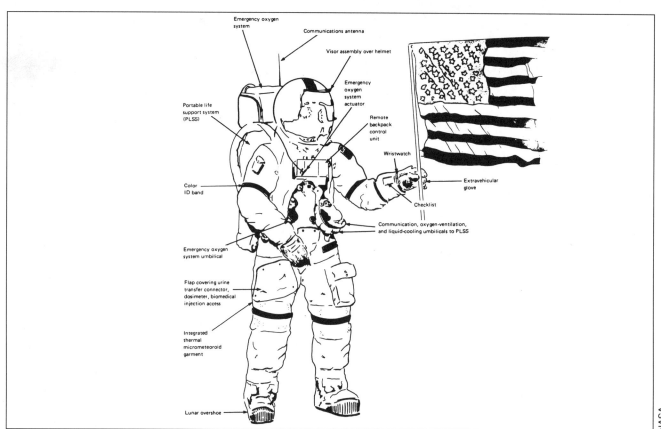

Space suit for walking on the Moon

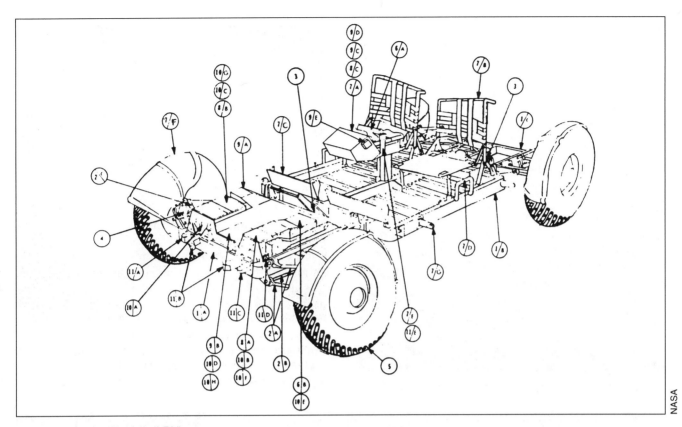

The Lunar Roving Vehicle (LRV)

missions, this spacecraft carried a strange four-wheeled jitney stashed away in the Lunar Module Descent Stage. The Lunar Roving Vehicle (LRV or "Rover" for short) revolutionized the ability of astronauts to get around on the Moon's surface.

Astronauts David Scott and LM pilot James Irwin took the LM "Falcon" to the lunar surface to spend three days near Hadley Rille. They spent nearly 21 hours walking the surface of the Moon or using the Rover. Alfred Worden had the lonely duty of piloting the CSM "Endeavor," but Worden had an opportunity for an EVA from the CSM, recovering materials from an experiment bay in the Endeavor's Service Module. His space walk lasted 38 minutes, 12 seconds. The Apollo 15 crew's total flight time was 12 days, seven hours, 12 minutes, and they splashed down in the Pacific on August 7 with 173 pounds of moon rocks.

Apollo 16: Cartesian Roving

While other Apollo explorers had sampled the basaltic basins of the Moon's *maria* (literally "seas," or broad, flat plains where long ago volcanoes had formed rocks called basalts), and taken a close look at a mountain range, John Young, Thomas Mattingly and Charles Duke set out on Apollo 16 to explore a new area—the Descartes highlands. The light color of this area contrasted with the darker *maria*, and geologists thought the composition of the rocks would be quite different.

Unfortunately, the CSM "Casper" developed engine troubles, which delayed lunar landing and shortened the mission by a day.

Duke and Young did land the LM "Orion," however, near the crater Descartes. During EVAs lasting 20 hours, 14 minutes they collected a record 213 pounds of lunar samples and trekked 16.8 miles (27 km) in the Rover.

The two used an ultraviolet camera set on a tripod for making some astronomical observations, drilled for deep core samples, attempted to set up detectors to measure heat flow, and set out both a passive and active seismic experiment. They discovered that the Descartes crater was magnetized and found a glass prism that indicated intense heating in the past—two clues that added to the mosaic of information being amassed about the Moon.

The penultimate Apollo mission splashed down in the Pacific April 27 after a total flight time of 11 days, one hour, 51 minutes.

Apollo 15 view of the moon

Apollo 17: Geologist on the Moon

With the launch of Apollo 17 on December 7, 1972, the Apollo saga would come to an end. This was the sixth and last manned landing on the Moon and the third with the lunar rover. Eugene Cernan, Ron Evans and geologist Harrison Schmitt were on board—the first time any professional scientist had a chance to travel beyond our planet to examine another body in our solar system firsthand.

After separating from the CM "Challenger," Cernan and Schmitt landed the LM "America" near the Taurus Mountains and in the following three days they spent a total of 22 hours, four minutes each in a total of three EVAs. They set up several experiments and Schmitt followed a hunch that he'd find evidence of a history of volcanic activity in the area. A piece of orange glass the astronauts found later proved not to be volcanic, however. The mission lasted 11 days, 13 hours, 51 minutes, and brought back 243 pounds of lunar samples. The Apollo 17 splashed down at 2:24 P.M. EST in the Pacific Ocean on November 19, 1972. Apollo hardware would be used for a couple more

Apollo 16 Rover or Lunar Roving Vehicle (LRV) at Plum Crater on the Moon, April 21, 1972

NASA

Gene Cernan driving the Rover during Apollo 17 mission to the Moon

NASA

Geologist Harrison Schmitt checks out a boulder on the Moon's surface during an Apollo 17 EVA

years in two innovative programs—Skylab and the joint Soviet-U.S. Apollo-Soyuz Test Project—but Apollo's series of breathtaking, fantastic voyages to the Moon had come to an end.

Combined, the Apollo astronauts had carried back 847.2 pounds (384.2 kg) of samples of lunar soil and rock. While Apollo did answer some questions about the Moon and gave scientists a great deal of data to examine, the mysterious origin of the Moon still stirs up controversy. Some scientists believe that the only way to really settle the question will be to go back and take another look.

Meanwhile, having faced the major disappointments in 1971 of the frustrated Soyuz 10 mission and the tragedy of Soyuz 11, the Soviets were gearing up their new Salyut space station. They had shown that their Salyut station could support a long-duration mission of up to 23 days. While their first successful mission was still a ways off at the end of 1972, they were moving ahead, like the U.S., toward a new era in space.

It would be an era in which literally hundreds of satellites would dot the skies, performing dozens of tasks. Nation after nation would join in the business, scientific and military enterprise of the exploration of space. It would see the United States develop a "Shuttle" system that would carry crews of five to seven astronauts and mission specialists into orbit to work. It would foster lofty dreams of space stations and space planes, of space communities and lunar colonies, and missions to Mars.

Already in November 1972 both Soviets and Americans had made ingenious technological breakthroughs, overcome enormous physical obstacles, braved tragedy and disappointment and achieved heroic feats. We had established our first human toehold in space and had truly begun to climb out of the cradle provided by the resources and atmosphere of our planet Earth. We had started our journey outward, through the universe.

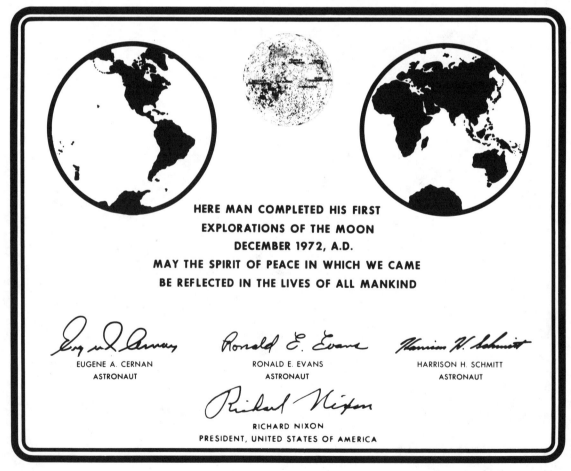

HERE MAN COMPLETED HIS FIRST
EXPLORATIONS OF THE MOON
DECEMBER 1972, A.D.
MAY THE SPIRIT OF PEACE IN WHICH WE CAME
BE REFLECTED IN THE LIVES OF ALL MANKIND

EUGENE A. CERNAN
ASTRONAUT

RONALD E. EVANS
ASTRONAUT

HARRISON H. SCHMITT
ASTRONAUT

RICHARD NIXON
PRESIDENT, UNITED STATES OF AMERICA

NASA

Plaque attached to the ladder of the Apollo 17 Lunar Module Challenger's descent stage left on the moon

APPENDIX

PIONEERS IN SPACE

Summary of people who made missions to space through 1972

Vostok 1 (USSR)	Gagarin	April 12, 1961
Mercury-Redstone 3 (U.S.)	Shepard	May 5, 1961
Mercury-Redstone 4 (U.S.)	Grissom	July 21, 1961
Vostok 2 (USSR)	Titov	August 6-7, 1961
Mercury-Atlas 6 (U.S.)	Glenn	Feb 20, 1962
Mercury-Atlas 7 (U.S.)	Carpenter	May 24, 1962
Vostok 3 (USSR)	Nikolayev	Aug 11-15, 1962
Vostok 4 (USSR)	Popovich	Aug 12-15, 1962
Mercury-Atlas 8 (U.S.)	Schirra	Oct 3, 1962
Mercury-Atlas 9 (U.S.)	Cooper	May 15-16, 1963
Vostok 5 (USSR)	Bykovsky	June 14-19, 1963
Vostok 6 (USSR)	Tereshkova	June 16-19, 1963
Voskhod 1 (USSR)	Komarov, Yegorov, Feoktistov	Oct 12-13, 1964
Voskhod 2 (USSR)	Belyayev, Leonov	March 18-19, 1965
Gemini 3 (U.S.)	Grissom, Young	March 23, 1965
Gemini 4 (U.S.)	McDivitt, White	June 3-7, 1965
Gemini 5 (U.S.)	Cooper, Conrad	Aug 21-29, 1965
Gemini 7 (U.S.)	Borman, Lovell	Dec 4-18, 1965
Gemini 6-A (U.S.)	Schirra, Stafford	Dec 15-16, 1965
Gemini 8 (U.S.)	Armstrong, Scott	Mar 16, 1966
Gemini 9-A (U.S.)	Stafford, Cernan	June 3-6, 1966
Gemini 10 (U.S.)	Young, Collins	July 18-21, 1966
Gemini 11 (U.S.)	Conrad, Gordon	Sept 12-15, 1966
Gemini 12 (U.S.)	Lovell, Aldrin	Nov 11-15, 1966
Soyuz 1 (USSR)	Komarov (died on reentry)	April 23-24, 1967
Apollo-Saturn 7 (U.S.)	Schirra, Eisele, Cunningham	Oct 11-22, 1968
Soyuz 3 (USSR)	Beregovoy	Oct 26-30, 1968
Apollo-Saturn 8 (U.S.)	Borman, Lovell, Anders	Dec 21-27, 1968
Soyuz 4 (USSR)	Shatalov	Jan 14-17, 1969
Soyuz 5 (USSR)	Volynov, Yeliseyev, Khrunov	Jan 15-18, 1969
Apollo-Saturn 9 (U.S.)	McDivitt, Scott, Schweickart	March 3-13, 1969
Apollo-Saturn 10 (U.S.)	Stafford, Young, Cernan	May 18-26, 1969
Apollo-Saturn 11 (U.S.)	Armstrong, Collins, Aldrin	July 16-24, 1969
Soyuz 6 (USSR)	Shonin, Kubasov	Oct 11-16, 1969
Soyuz 7 (USSR)	Filipchenko, Volkov, Gorbatko	Oct 12-17, 1969
Soyuz 8 (USSR)	Shatalov, Yeliseyev	Oct 13-18, 1969
Apollo-Saturn 12 (U.S.)	Conrad, Gordon, Bean	Nov 14-24, 1969
Apollo-Saturn 13 (U.S.)	Lovell, Swigert, Haise	April 11-17, 1970
Soyuz 9 (USSR)	Nikolayev, Sevastyanov	June 1-19, 1970
Apollo-Saturn 14 (U.S.)	Shepard, Roosa, Mitchell	Jan 31-Feb 9, 1971
Soyuz 10 (USSR)	Shatalov, Yeliseyev, Rukavishnikov	April 23-25, 1971
Soyuz 11 (USSR)	Dobrovolsky, Volkov, Patsayev (died during reentry)	June 6-30, 1971
Apollo-Saturn 15 (U.S.)	Scott, Worden, Irwin	July 26-Aug 7, 1971
Apollo-Saturn 16 (U.S.)	Young, Mattingly, Duke	April 16-27, 1972
Apollo-Saturn 17 (U.S.)	Cernan, Evans, Schmitt	Dec 7-19, 1972

GLOSSARY

abort To end a mission or activity prematurely (before planned completion).

aerodynamics The branch of science that studies the behavior and flow of air around objects, and the forces it exerts on those objects, including resistance or drag, pressure, etc.

Agena An upper-stage rocket booster used during Gemini missions as a docking target vehicle.

Apollo The NASA project that landed 12 men on the Moon between 1969 and 1972.

Atlas rocket The rocket that powered the launches of Project Mercury missions. Originally designed as an ICBM (a military missile).

attitude The position of a spacecraft in flight in relation to a fixed reference such as the horizon or another vehicle.

ballistic descent A flight path that returns a spacecraft to Earth in the same manner as a bullet or other falling object.

ballistic trajectory The curved path of a projectile, such as a ballistic missile or a bullet, after the thrust or propelling force has ended. Because early spacecraft like Mercury, Vostok and so on had very little control, they had to be aligned exactly right at launch in order to enter orbit properly. They traveled along ballistic trajectories.

basaltic Describes a type of rock formed when molten magma (e.g., from an erupting volcano) solidifies—found in many areas both on the Earth and the Moon.

booster In a multistage rocket, any of the rockets that provide the early stages of propulsion, including the initial stage that provides power for the launching and initial part of the flight.

Cape Canaveral The Air Force station from which all Mercury and Gemini missions were launched as well as, to this day, most unmanned missions. Called Cape Kennedy between 1963 and 1973.

CM The Command Module, one of the three main parts of the Apollo spacecraft. Shaped like a cone, it contained the crew quarters, and was the only portion of the spacecraft that returned to Earth at the completion of a mission.

CSM The Command/Service Module (Command Module and Service Module combined) of the Apollo spacecraft.

Cold War After World War II, an extended period of animosity between the U.S.S.R. and the U.S., when the countries were hostile and uncooperative with each other, even though not at war.

combustion Rapid oxidation or burning.

deflectable vanes Movable devices located in the nozzle at the rear of a rocket engine. These vanes could be used to control or guide the path of the rocket by changing the direction that exhaust gases flowed through the nozzle.

Delta rocket A booster rocket used primarily to launch small- to medium-sized satellites into Earth orbit.

docking When two spacecraft connect or "link up" with each other while in orbit.

docking adaptor An apparatus that makes it possible for one spacecraft to link up with another.

EVA Extravehicular activity—a spacewalk or moonwalk.

exhaust stream The stream or jet of gases expelled by burning rocket fuel.

exhaust velocity The speed of the gases expelled as the rocket fuel burns.

flight trajectory The path traveled by a flying object, such as a rocket or spacecraft.

free-return trajectory A flight path that takes advantage of natural gravitational forces, enabling a return to Earth without use of rocket engines.

Gemini NASA's second manned space project, lasting from 1965-1966. The Gemini spacecraft (the name means "Twins") carried two astronauts on each mission.

gyroscopic control and stabilization The use of a gyroscope (a device used for maintaining stability in ships and airplanes) to automatically keep a craft in the proper relative position or attitude.

high definition Describes an image having a very clear, sharp focus and showing fine detail. For example, the high-definition photos from a Lunar Orbiter camera could show details as small as 3 feet from an altitude of 18,000 feet.

ICBM An inter-continental ballistic missile, a military rocket carrying a nuclear warhead and designed to travel at least 3,000 miles. The rocket power of the ICBM formed the foundation for both U.S. and Soviet space programs.

Industrial Revolution A time during the 19th century when the replacement of hand tools by power tools and mechanized production brought about widespread social and economic change.

JPL Jet Propulsion Laboratory, in Pasadena, California. A NASA research laboratory, transferred from Army jurisdiction to NASA in 1958, and operated in conjunction with the California Institute of Technology. JPL managed the (unmanned) Ranger and Surveyor missions to the Moon.

JSC Johnson Space Center, the NASA center at Clear Lake, Texas, near Houston. Previously known as the Manned Spacecraft Center, this site houses NASA Mission Control, which manages all manned spaceflights after lift-off from Cape Canaveral Air Force Station (Mercury, Gemini, and most unmanned missions) or from Kennedy Space Center (Apollo missions and, later, Skylab and Shuttle missions).

KSC Kennedy Space Center, the NASA center on Merritt Island in Florida from which all Apollo missions were launched.

keeping station Maneuvering a spacecraft so that it remains near another object in orbit.

kinetic theory of gases A theory describing the constant motion of minute particles of all matter.

LM The Lunar Module, one of the three main parts of the Apollo spacecraft, used to land astronauts on the Moon.

Landsat Name given to a series of Earth observation satellites.

liquid fuel A fuel, such as liquid oxygen (LOX), that burns in a liquid state.

lift-off Ascent of a spacecraft from the launch pad (at least two inches).

Mercury The NASA project that included the first U.S. manned missions into space.

Mexican War The war fought between the U.S. and Mexico from 1846 to 1848.

mooring latches Hardware used to fasten two spacecraft when docking.

multistage rocket Several rockets fired in combination to achieve greater heights.

nitroglycerin A highly explosive substance used in dynamite.

nozzle The opening at the rear of a rocket engine through which exhaust gases flow.

orbital maneuvering system A system or set of mechanisms for maneuvering a spacecraft in orbit or from one orbit to another.

oxidizer A material that supplies oxygen so that combustion can take place in a rocket engine.

parking orbit An orbit where an object can be left safely for a period of time.

passive communications satellite A satellite (such as the Echo series) that just reflects signals from its surface, without originating any signals.

payload Anything that's not part of the functioning of a rocket or spacecraft but is transported by it to carry out a purpose or mission. For example, Ham the chimpanzee was a payload aboard an early Mercury test flight; Ranger missions carried cameras and other instruments to collect and report back data about the Moon.

projectile Any object propelled forward by a force. For example, a bullet or a spacecraft.

propulsion A force that propels, or pushes, an object forward.

rendezvous When two spacecraft in orbit are brought almost close enough together to touch.

retrofire Firing rockets in the opposite direction from the direction of flight to slow a spacecraft (a procedure used during reentry).

retropack A system of auxiliary rockets (retro- rockets) on a spacecraft, used to reduce speed by firing in the oposite direction from the direction of travel.

retro-rockets Rockets used to slow the speed of a spacecraft. They are fired in the opposite direction from the direction of flight ("retro-" or backward) to bring the spacecraft back into the atmosphere.

shroud A shell or cover that protects a spacecraft or mechanism from the heat of launching.

stabilizing drogue parachute A small parachute used to steady the flight of the spacecraft during reentry. This parachute then pulls out the main parachute to slow the spacecraft's descent.

SM The Service Module, one of the three main parts of the Apollo spacecraft. Cylindrical in shape, it contained fuel, supplies and engines.

Saturn rocket A powerful, giant rocket designed to send Apollo missions to the Moon.

solid fuel A fuel, such as gunpowder, that is a solid (as opposed to being in a liquid or a gaseous state). Solid-fuel rocket repellant resembles a rubber eraser in appearance and requires high heat to ignite.

sounding rocket A rocket used to obtain information about the atmosphere.

Soyuz A Soviet spacecraft originally designed to carry three cosmonauts. Its name, meaning "union,"

indicates its main mission, to provide transportation to and from a space station, where it would dock during missions aboard the station. The descendents of this spacecraft, the Soyuz TM series, are still being flown today.

speed of sound At 32 degrees F (0 degrees C) the speed of sound in air is about 760 mph (332 meters per second).

suborbital Describes a flight that did not make an orbit around the Earth, such as Alan Shepard's Mercury flight.

subsonic Slower than the speed of sound.

supersonic Faster than the speed of sound.

thrust The push forward caused in reaction to a high-speed jet of fluid or gases discharged in the opposite direction from a rocket's nozzle.

thrusters Rocket engines, especially those used for maneuvering a spacecraft.

upper stage In a multistage rocket, a booster rocket that takes over after the first-stage rocket has burned its fuel.

venting out Expelling a gas.

Voskhod A modified Soviet Vostok spacecraft, used for two manned missions in 1964-65. Its name means "ascent" or "sunrise."

Vostok The first manned Soviet spacecraft. Its name means "East."

window of opportunity The space of time during whcih an action can be taken successfully, such as a window of opportunity for a launch or for a descent from orbit.

yawing A sideways swing of a spacecraft.

SUGGESTIONS FOR FURTHER READING

Aldrin, Edwin E., Jr. *Return to Earth*. New York: Random House, 1973.

Armstrong, Neil, Michael Collins, and Edwin E. Aldrin, Jr., et al. *First on the Moon*. Boston: Little, Brown and Co., Inc. 1970.

Ash, Brian, ed. *The Visual Encyclopedia of Science Fiction*. New York: Harmony Books, 1977.

Associated Press. *Moments in Space*. New York: Gallery Books, 1986.

Baker, David. *The History of Manned Space Flight, Revised Edition*. New York: Crown Publishers, Inc., 1982.

———. *The Rocket: The History and Development of Rocket & Missile Technology*. New York: Crown Publishers, Inc., 1978.

Benford, Timothy B., and Brian Wilkes. *The Space Program Quiz & Fact Book*. New York: Harper & Row, 1985.

Bergaust, Erik. *Reaching for the Stars*. New York: Doubleday, 1960.

———. *Rocket City, USA*. New York: Macmillan, 1963.

Bond, Peter. *Heroes in Space: From Gagarin to Challenger*. New York: Basil Blackwell, Inc. 1987.

Borman, Frank, with Robert J. Serling. *Countdown: An Autobiography*. New York: Silver Arrow Books, 1988.

Cassutt, Michael. *Who's Who in Space: The First 25 Years*. Boston: G.K. Hall & Co., 1987.

Clark, Phillip. *The Soviet Manned Space Program: An Illustrated History of the Men, the Missions, and the Spacecraft*. New York: Orion Books, 1988.

Collins, Michael. *Carrying the Fire: An Astronaut's Journey*. New York: Farrar, Straus & Giroux, 1974.

———. *Liftoff: The Story of America's Adventure in Space*. New York: Grove Press, 1988.

Cortright, Edgar M., Ed. *Apollo Expeditions to the Moon*. Washington, D.C.: NASA, 1975.

Dewaard, E. John and Nancy. *History of NASA: America's Voyage to the Stars*. New York: Exeter Books, 1984.

Gatland, Kenneth, et al. *The Illustrated Encyclopedia of Space Technology: A Comprehensive History of Space Exploration*. New York: Harmony Books, 1981.

Grissom, Betty, and Henry Still. *Starfall*. New York: Crowell, 1974.

Grissom, Virgil I. *Gemini: A Personal Account of Man's Venture into Space*. New York: Macmillan, 1968.

Hart, Douglas. *The Encyclopedia of Soviet Spacecraft*. New York: Exeter Books, 1987.

Hurt, Harry, III. *For All Mankind*. New York: Atlantic Monthly Press, 1988.

Johnson, Nicholas L. *Handbook of Soviet Manned Space Flight*. San Diego: Univelt, Inc., 1980.

Kerrod, Robin. *The Illustrated History of NASA*. New York: Gallery Books, 1986.

Lehman, Milton. *This High Man: The Life of Robert H. Goddard*. New York: Farrar, Straus & Co., 1963.

Ley, Willie. *Rockets, Missiles and Space Travel*. New York: Viking, 1961.

McAleer, Neil. *The Omni Space Almanac*. New York: World Almanac, 1987.

McDougall, Walter A. *. . . the Heavens and the Earth: A Political History of the Space Age*. New York: Basic Books, Inc., 1985.

Nicholls, Peter, Ed. *The Science Fiction Encyclopedia*. Garden City, New York: Dolphin Books, 1979.

Oberg, James E. *Red Star in Orbit: The Inside Story of Soviet Failures and Triumphs in Space*. New York: Random House, 1981.

Ordway, Frederick I., III and Mitchell R. Sharpe. *The Rocket Team.* New York: Thomas Y. Crowell, 1979.

Schirra, Walter M., Jr., with Richard N. Billings. *Schirra's Space.* Boston: Quinlan Press, 1988.

Shepard, Alan B., Jr., Virgil I. Grissom, John H. Glenn, Jr., M. Scott Carpenter, Walter M. Schirra, Jr., L. Gordon Cooper., Jr., and Donald K. Slayton. *We Seven.* New York: Simon & Schuster, 1962.

Silvestri, Goffredo, et al. *Quest for Space: Man's Greatest Adventure—The Facts, the Machines, the Technology.* Trans. Simon Pleasance. New York: Crescent Books, 1987.

Smolders, Peter. *Soviets in Space.* Trans. Marian Powell. New York: Taplinger Publishing Co., Inc., 1974.

Swenson, Loyd S., Jr., et al. *This New Ocean: A History of Project Mercury.* The NASA Historical Series. Washington, D.C.: NASA, 1966.

Tsiolkovsky, K. E. *Selected Works.* Trans. G. Yankovsky. Moscow: Mir Publishers, 1968.

Von Braun, Wernher, et al. *Space Travel: A History.* An update (and Fourth Edition) of *History of Rocketry & Space Travel.* New York: Harper & Row, 1985.

Williams, Beryl, and Samuel Epstein. *The Rocket Pioneers on the Road to Space.* New York: Julian Messner, Inc., 1955.

Wolfe, Tom. *The Right Stuff.* New York: Farrar, Straus & Giroux, 1979.

Yeager, Chuck, and Leo Janos. *Yeager—An Autobiography.* New York: Bantam Books, 1985.

Yenne, Bill. *The Astronauts: The First 25 Years of Manned Space Flight.* New York: Exeter Books, 1986.

———. *The Encyclopedia of U.S. Spacecraft.* New York: Exeter Books, 1985.

INDEX

A-1 rocket, 15, 18
A-2 rocket, 15, 18
A-3 rocket, 16, 18
A-4 rocket, *See* V-2 rocket
A-5 rocket, 16, 18
A-10 rocket, 16
Able (monkey), 32, 43
Adams, Michael, 40-41
Aerobee rocket, 22
Aerojet Corporation, 20
Agena Target Vehicle, 57, 58-62, 64, 80, 102
Aldrin, Edwin "Buzz," 62-63, 64, 77, 87-88, 90-93, 101
America, *See* Apollo command module
American Interplanetary Society, *See* American Rocket Society
American Rocket Society, 13, 15, 18, 21, 25
Amy (mouse), 33, 43
Anders, William, 74, 77, 101
Antares, *See* Apollo lunar module
Apollo program, 45, 48, 55, 56, 62, 65-66, 67-68, 69-78, 81, 87-100, 102; Apollo 1, 62, 65-66, 67-68, 70, 72,. 77, 92; Apollo 4, 71, 77, 101; Apollo 5, 71, 77, 101; Apollo 6, 71, 77, 101; Apollo 7, 66, 71- 72, 74, 77, 79, 101; Apollo 8, 69, 74-75, 77, 80, 88, 90, 101; Apollo 9, 76, 77, 101; Apollo 10, 76-77, 87, 88, 101; Apollo 11, 77, 87-88, 90-93, 94, 101; Apollo 12, 77, 94, 101; Apollo 13, 77, 94-95, 101; Apollo 14, 48, 78, 95-96, 101; Apollo 15, 78, 96-97, 98, 101; Apollo 16, 78, 97, 98, 101; Apollo 17, 78, 98-100, 101
Apollo command module, 61, 63, 65, 72, 75, 77, 89, 94, 102; design of spacecraft, 73-74, 88, 89-91; America, 98; Casper, 78, 97; Charlie Brown, 76-77; Columbia, 77, 87, 92; Endeavor, 97; Gumdrop, 76, 77; Kitty Hawk, 96; Odyssey, 77
Apollo command service module, *See* Apollo command module
Apollo lunar module, 63, 73-74, 77, 89-90; design of spacecraft, 89- 90; Antares, 78, 95-96; Aquarius, 78, 94; Challenger, 98, 100; Eagle, 77, 87-88; 91-93; Falcon, 97; Intrepid, 94; Orion, 97; Snoopy, 76-77; Spider, 76, 77
Apollo-Saturn, *See* Apollo
Apollo-Soyuz Test Project, 48, 100
Apt, Milburn, 38, 40

Aquarius, *See* Apollo lunar module
Ariosto, Lodovico, 4
Aristotle, ix
Armstrong, Neil, 58-59, 60, 64, 77, 87-88, 90-93, 101
Artmeyev, Vladimir, 23, 27
Atlas Able 4, 33
Atlas Able 5A, 33
Atlas Able 5B, 33
Atlas rocket, 22, 23, 31, 32, 44, 46, 51, 57, 60, 102
Aurora 7, *See* Mercury 7

Babylonians, 3
Bacon, Roger, 6
Baikonur cosmodrome, 28
Baker (monkey), 32, 43
Bassett, Charles, 59, 64
bazooka, 10, 26
Bean, Alan, 77, 94, 101
Belka (dog), 33, 43
Bell Telephone Laboratories, 32
Belyayev, Pavel, 53-55, 101
Beregovoy, Georgy, 79, 83, 101
Bergerac, Savinien de Cyrano de, 4
Boeing Aerospace, 70
Borman, Frank, 58, 63, 74, 77, 101
Brezhnev, Leonid, 53
British Interplanetary Society, 13, 21
Bumper rocket program, *See* Project Bumper
Bykovsky, Valery, 47, 49, 66, 101

California Institute of Technology, 25, 26, 30
Caltech, *See* California Institute of Technology
Canaveral, Cape, 26, 30, 32, 37, 43, 44, 102
Carpenter, Malcolm Scott, 42, 47, 48, 49, 51, 101
Casper, *See* Apollo command module
Cernan, Eugene, 59, 61, 64, 76-77, 78, 87, 98-99, 101
Chaffee, Roger, 65-66, 67, 71, 77, 92
Challenger, *See* Apollo lunar module
Charlie Brown, *See* Apollo command module
Chernushka (dog), 43-49
China (rocket development), 6
Civil War, American, 7
CM, *See* Apollo command module
Cold War, 25, 102

Colliers magazine, 26
Collins, Michael, 52, 60, 64, 77, 87-88, 92-93, 101
Columbia, *See* Apollo command module
Congreve, William, 6, 7
Conrad, Charles "Pete," 58, 60-61, 63, 64, 77, 94, 101
Cooper, Leroy Gordon, 42, 48, 49, 51, 58, 63, 101
Corporal E rocket, 26
Courier 1B satellite, 32, 33
Cronkite, Walter, 47
Crossfield, Scott, 37, 38, 39, 40
CSM, *See* Apollo command module
Cunningham, Walter, 72, 74, 77, 101

Dana, William, 40-41
Delta rocket, 102
Descartes crater, *See* Moon
Discoverer satellites, 31
Dobrovolsky, Georgy, 82, 84, 101
docking (spacecraft), 59-62, 64, 76
Dornberger, Walter, 13, 15-17, 18, 19
Douglas skyrocket, 38
Duke, Charles, 78, 97, 101

Eagle, *See* Apollo lunar module
Early Bird satellite, 63
Echo 1, 32, 33
Edwards Air Force Base, 37-40
Eisele, Donn, 72, 77, 101
Eisenhower, Dwight D., 17, 23, 26, 30, 45
Emme, Eugene M., 12
Endeavor, *See* Apollo command module
Engle, Joe, 40-41
Enos (chimpanzee), 46, 49
Esnault-Pelterie, Robert, 17, 27
EVA, *See* extravehicular activity
Evans, Ronald, 78, 98, 101
Everest, Pat, Jr., 38
Explorer 1 satellite, 30-31, 32, 44
Explorer 2, 30, 32
Explorer 3, 32
Explorer 6, 31
extravehicular activity (EVA), 53-55, 56-57, 59, 60, 61, 68, 76, 78, 80, 88, 90-91, 94, 96, 97, 98-100, 102

FAI, *See* Fédération Astronautique Internationale
Faith 7, *See* Mercury 9
Falcon, *See* Apollo lunar module
Fédération Astronautique Internationale, 41
Feoktistov, Konstantin, 52, 63, 101
Filipchenko, Anatoly, 81, 83, 101

Fra Mauro, *See* Moon
Freedom 7, *See* Mercury 3
Friendship 7, *See* Mercury 6

Gagarin, Yuri, 27, 42, 44, 45, 49, 50, 67, 79, 92, 101
GALCIT, 25
Galilei, Galileo, ix
Gas Dynamics Laboratory, *See* GDL
GDL, 24, 27
GDL-OKB, 28
Gemini program, 45, 48, 55-64, 65, 70, 87; design of spacecraft, 56- 57; Gemini 1, 55, 63; Gemini 2, 55, 63; Gemini 3, 55-56, 63, 67; Gemini 4, 56, 59, 63; Gemini 5, 58, 63; Gemini 6, 57, 58, 63; Gemini 6A, *See* Gemini 6; Gemini 7, 57, 58, 63, 81; Gemini 8, 57, 58- 59, 60, 64, 87; Gemini 9, 59-60, 64; Gemini 9A, *See* Gemini 9; Gemini 10, 52, 60, 64, 87; Gemini 11, 60-61, 64; Gemini 12, 62-63, 64, 87
General Electric Corporation, 22
GIRD, 13, 27
Girl in the Moon, 14, 15, 18
Glamorous Glennis, 39
Glenn, John, 42, 46-47, 49, 51, 101
Glennan, T. Keith, 29
Glushko, Valentin, 26, 27
Goddard, Esther, 12
Goddard, Robert, 6, 10-12, 13, 14, 20, 21, 24, 25-26, 27
Goddard Space Flight Center, 12
Gorbatko, Viktor, 81, 83, 101
Gordon, Richard, 60-61, 64, 77, 94, 101
Grave, D. A., 27
Grissom, Virgil "Gus," 42, 45, 49, 55-56, 57, 63, 64, 65-67, 71, 77, 92, 101
Grottrüp, Helmut, 17, 24-25, 28
Group for the Study of Reactive Propulsion, *See* GIRD
Guggenheim Foundation, 12, 25
Gumdrop, *See* Apollo command module

Hadley Apennine mountains, *See* Moon
Hadley Rille, *See* Moon
Haise, Fred, 78, 94-95, 101
Ham (chimpanzee), 43-44, 49
Hermes rocket, 22
high-velocity aircraft rockets (HVARs), 25
Hitler, Adolph, 15
Hohmann, Walter, 17
HVAR, *See* high-velocity aircraft rockets

IGY, *See* International Geophysical Year
International Geophysical Year, 23, 25

Intelsat 1, *See* Early Bird
Intrepid, *See* Apollo lunar module
Irwin, James, 78, 97, 101

JATO, *See* jet-assisted takeoff
jet-assisted takeoff, 26, 27
Jet Propulsion Laboratory, 20, 21, 22, 25-26, 30, 31
Johnson, Lyndon B., 31, 56
JPL, *See* Jet Propulsion Laboratory
Juno 1 rocket, 30, 32
Jupiter C rocket, 26, 30, 32

Kegeldüse, 15, 18
Kennedy, Cape, 48, 77, 102
Kennedy, John F., 55, 63, 82
Kennedy Space Center, 75, 87
Kepler, Johannes, 4
Key, Francis Scott, 7
Khrunov, Yevgeny, 66, 80, 83, 101
Khruschev, Nikita, 33, 44, 45, 52-53, 55
Kincheloe, Ivan C., 38
Kitty Hawk, 10, 25
Knight, William, 40-41
Komarov, Vladimir, 52, 63, 66-67, 68, 79, 80, 83, 92, 101
Kondratyuk, Yuri, 26, 27
Korolev, Sergei, 24, 27, 28, 49-50, 52-55, 79
Kramarov, G. M., 27
KSC, *See* Kennedy Space Center
Kubasov, Valery, 81, 83, 101

Laika (dog), 29, 43
Lang, Fritz, 14, 18
Lenin, Vladimir, 23, 26
Leonov, Alexei, 53-55, 56, 57, 59, 63, 101
Ley, Willie, 18
Liberty Bell 7, *See* Mercury 4
Life magazine, 47
Lindbergh, Charles, 46
liquid fuel rockets, 11-12, 18, 24, 25, 27
LM, *See* Apollo lunar module
Lockheed Missles and Space Company, 61
Lovell, James, 58, 62, 63, 64, 69, 74, 77, 78, 94-95, 101
Luce, Clare Boothe, 47
Lucian of Samosata, 4
Luna 2, 32
Luna 3, 32
Luna 9, 63
Luna 10, 64
Luna 15, 92

Luna lunar lander series, 33, 74
Lunar Orbiter spacecraft, 70-71
lunar rover, *See* lunar roving vehicle
lunar roving vehicle, 78, 90, 97

Mach 1, 37, 38
Mach 2, 38
Mach 3, 38
Magnus, Albert, 6
Manhattan Project, 22
Mariner 4, 63
Mars, 33, 44, 63, 100
Marshall Spaceflight Center, 22, 31
Mattingly, Thomas "Ken," 78, 94, 97, 101
McDivitt, James, 56-58, 63, 76, 77, 101
McDonnell Douglass Aircraft Corporation, 51, 57, 59, 70
McKay, John, 40-41
Mercury program, 31, 32, 33, 41, 42-51, 52, 65, 70, 87, 96, 102, 104; design of spacecraft, 50-51, 57; Mercury 2, 49; Mercury 3, 44-45, 49, 51, 55, 96, 101; Mercury 4, 45, 49, 51, 56, 67; Mercury 5, 46, 49; Mercury 6, 46-47, 49, 51; Mercury 7, 47, 49, 51; Mercury 8, 48, 49, 51; Mercury 9, 48, 49, 51
"Mercury Seven" astronauts, 32, 37, 42, 96
Merritt Island, 103
Mexican War, 7
Midas 2 satellite, 32, 33
Miss Sam (monkey), 43
Mitchell, Edgar, 78, 96, 101
Moe (mouse), 33, 43
Mojave Desert, California, 37-40
Molly Brown, *See* Gemini 3
Moon, color, 92, 97; craters, 74; interior, 97, 98; landing sites, 74, 96; maria, 97; rocks, 78, 100; surface features: Apennine mountains, *See* Hadley Apennines; Descartes crater, 78, 97; Descartes highlands, 96, 97; Fra Mauro, 77, 78, 95-96; Hadley Apennines, 96; Hadley Rille, 78, 97; Ocean of Storms, 63, 77, 94, 96; Sea of Tranquility, 88, 92, 96; Taurus-Littrow, 96; Taurus mountains, 98
Mushka (dog), 33, 43

NACA, *See* National Advisory Committee for Aeronautics
National Advisory Committee for Aeronautics, 31
National Aeronautics and Space Administration (NASA), 12, 31, 32, 37, 39, 41, 42, 44, 56, 57, 63, 65-66, 71, 76, 102
NASA, *See* National Aeronautics and Space Administration

Naval Research Laboratory, 26, 30
Nazi political party, 15-17
Nebel, Rudolf, 17, 18
Nedelin disaster, 44, 45
Nedelin, Mitrofan, 44
Nesmeyanov, A. N., 20
New York Times, 11, 12
Newton's Third Law of Motion, 9
Nikolayev, Andrian, 47, 49, 81, 84, 101
North American Aviation, 30

Oberth, Hermann, 12, 13-15, 17, 18, 24, 27
Ocean of Storms, *See* Moon
Odyssey, *See* Apollo command module
Old Reliable (monkey), 43
Operation Paperclip, 17, 19, 26
ORDCIT, 21
Orion, *See* Apollo lunar module
ORM-1, 24, 27
ORM-2, 24

Patsayev, Viktor, 81, 84, 101
Peenemünde, 13, 16-17, 18, 19, 20, 26, 27
Pendray, Edward G., 15, 18, 25
Pendray, Lee Gregory, 15, 18, 25
Perelman, Y. I., 26, 27
Peterson, Forrest, 40
Petropavlovsky, B. S., 27
Pioneer 1, 32
Pioneer 2, 32
Pioneer 3, 32
Popovich, Pavel, 47, 49, 101
Private A rocket, 21
Private F rocket, 21
Project 212, 24, 27
Project Bumper, 22, 23, 26
Project Gemini, *See* Gemini program
Project Mercury *See* Mercury program
Project Score, 31, 32

quarantine, 93, 96

Ranger spacecraft, 33, 63, 70-71, 103
Raxumov, V. V., 27
Reaction Motors, Inc., 20, 26
Redstone Arsenal, 22-23
Redstone rocket, 22, 23, 43-45, 49, 51, 71
Reidel, Walter, 15, 18
rendezvous (spacecraft), 57, 58, 60-62, 64, 76, 79, 103
rocket development, 6-28

Rocketdyne, 70
Rocket-science Research institute, *See* RNII
Rockwell, 70
Roosa, Stuart, 78, 96, 101
RP-318-I rocket powered glider, 24, 27
Rukavishnikov, Nikolai, 82, 84, 101
Rushford, Robert, 40-41
Rynin, Nikolai A., 17, 27

Sally (mouse), 33, 43
Salyut space station, 80, 81, 100; Salyut 1, 82, 100
Sam (monkey), 43
Saturn I rocket, 77
Saturn IB rocket, 65, 71, 72, 77
Saturn IVB rocket, 69, 72
Saturn V rocket, 69, 71, 73, 74, 77, 87, 88, 89, 103
Schirra, Walter, 42, 48, 49, 51, 58, 63, 72, 77, 101
Schmitt, Harrison, 78, 98-99, 101
Schweickart, Russell "Rusty," 76, 77, 101
Scott, David, 58, 60, 64, 76, 77, 78, 97, 101
See, Elliott, 59, 64
Sevastyanov, Vitaly, 81, 84, 101
Shatalov, Vladimir, 80, 81, 82, 83, 84, 101
Shepard, Alan, 42, 44-45, 48, 49, 51, 55, 71, 78, 95-96, 101, 104
Shonin, Georgy, 81, 83, 101
Sigma 7, *See* Mercury 8
Skinner, L., 26
Skylab, 100
Slayton, Donald "Deke," 42, 48
Smithsonian Institution, 10-11, 12, 25
Snoopy, *See* Apollo lunar module
solid fuel rocket, 23, 24, 27
sonic barrier, 38
sonic boom, 38
sound barrier, 38
Soyuz program, 79-84, 103; Soyuz 1, 66-67, 68, 79, 83; Soyuz 2, 79, 83; Soyuz 3, 79, 83; Soyuz 4, 66, 79-80, 83; Soyuz 5, 66, 79-80, 83; Soyuz 6, 80, 83; Soyuz 7, 80, 83; Soyuz 8, 80, 83; Soyuz 9, 81, 84; Soyuz 10, 82, 84, 100; Soyuz 11, 82, 84, 100
Space Shuttle (U.S.), 37, 39, 41, 100
space sickness, 76
space station, 9, 26, 79, 100
space suit, 96
space travel, effects of, *See* weightlessness, effects of
space walk, *See* extravehicular activity
Spider, *See* Apollo lunar module
Sputnik 1, 25, 26, 29-31, 32
Sputnik 2, 29-30, 43
Sputnik 3, 30, 32
Sputnik 5, 33, 43

Sputnik 6, 43
Sputnik 9, 43, 49
Sputnik 10, 43
Stafford, Thomas, 58, 59, 61, 63, 64, 76-77, 87, 101
Stalin, Josef, 24, 28
Strelka (dog), 33, 43
Surveyor spacecraft, 70-71, 72
Surveyor 1, 64
Surveyor 3, 77, 94
Swigert, John, 78, 94-95, 101

Taurus-Littrow, *See* Moon
Tereshkova, Valentina, 47-48, 49, 81, 101
Thor rocket, 22
Tikhomirov, N. I., 23-24, 26, 27
TIROS 1, 31, 33
Titan rocket, 22, 57
Titov, Gherman, 45-46, 49
Tranquility, Sea of, *See* Moon
Transit 1B, 32, 33
Tsiolkovsky, Konstantin, 7-9, 11, 13, 23, 24, 27
Tyuratam, 28, 55, 80

V-1 flying bomb, 16, 24, 27
V-2 rocket, 13, 16-17, 18-19, 20-22, 25-26, 28
Valier, Max, 13-14, 17, 18-19, 27
Van Allen, James, 30
Van Allen Belts, 30
Vanguard rocket, 23, 26, 30-31, 32, 39, 42
Vanguard 1, 30
Vanguard 3, 31
Verein für Raumschiffart, 13-17, 18, 25
Verne, Jules, 4-5, 8, 13
Vetchinkin, V. P., 27
VfR, *See* Verein für Raumschiffart
Viking rocket, 22, 26
Volkov, Vladislav, 81, 82, 83, 84, 101
Volynov, Boris, 80, 83, 101
von Braun, Wernher, 13, 14, 15-17, 18, 19, 20-23, 26, 30, 31, 44, 69
von Opel, Fritz, 14, 18

Voskhod program, 52; design of spacecraft, 53-54, 104; Voskhod 1, 52- 53, 63; Voskhod 2, 53-55, 56, 59, 63
Vostok program, 42, 43, 44, 45-46, 47-48, 49-50, 52, 102; design of spacecraft, 49-50, 53, 104; Vostok 1, 42, 44, 49, 50; Vostok 2, 45- 46, 49; Vostok 3, 47, 49, 81; Vostok 4, 47, 49; Vostok 5, 47, 49; Vostok 6, 47-48, 49, 81

WAC-Corporal sounding rocket, 21-22, 26
Walker, Joe, 40-41
War of 1812, 6-7
weightlessness, effects of, 29, 42
Wells, H. G., 5
White, Edward, 56-58, 59, 63, 65-66, 67-68, 71, 77, 92, 101
White, Robert, 40-41
White Sands, New Mexico, 22, 26
Winkler, Johannes, 17, 18
women in space, 47-48, 50
Worden, Michael, 78, 97, 101
World War I, 10, 15, 18, 25
World War II, 12, 16-17, 18-19, 20, 24, 26
Wright brothers, 10, 25

X-1 rocket plane, 26, 37, 39
X-2 rocket plane, 38
X-15 rocket plane, 20, 37, 39-41, 42, 87

Yeager, Charles "Chuck," 26, 38
Yegorov, Boris, 52, 63, 101
Yeliseyev, Alexei, 66 80, 81, 82, 83, 84, 101
Young, John, 55-56, 57, 60, 63, 64, 67, 76-77, 78, 87, 97, 101

Ziegler, Skip, 38
Zond probes, 74, 79
Zvezdochka (dog), 43